RENEWABLE ENERGY

RENEWABLE ENERGY

A Concise Guide to Green Alternatives

JENNIFER CARLESS

Walker and Company
New York

First published in the United States of America in 1993 by Walker Publishing Company, Inc.

Published simultaneously in Canada by Thomas Allen & Son Canada, Limited, Markham, Ontario

Library of Congress Cataloging-in-Publication Data
Carless, Jennifer.
Renewable energy : a concise guide to green alternatives / Jennifer Carless.
p. cm.
Includes bibliographical references and index.
Summary: Discusses the availability, advantages, and environmental aspects of such alternative energy sources as solar power, wind energy, and hydropower.
ISBN 0-8027-8214-0
1. Renewable energy sources—United States.
[1. Renewable energy sources. 2. Power resources.] I. Title.
TJ807.9.U6C37 1993
333.79′4—dc20   92-35137
CIP
AC

Printed in the United States of America

2 4 6 8 10 9 7 5 3 1

THIS BOOK IS PRINTED ON RECYCLED PAPER

Contents

Foreword

Two events—less than two years and more than half a world apart—define the beginning of the end of the fossil-fuel age: the *Valdez* oil spill and the war in the Persian Gulf. In the aftermath of both, people were forced to redefine and reevaluate their relationship to the lifeblood of our modern society: oil. In Alaska, the myriad environmental impacts of oil were symbolized by those haunting images of slicked sea otters. In Iraq, the high-stakes politics that run beneath the global traffic in oil were laid bare—and the nature of oil as the currency of power was exposed. In each case we were forced to look at the central role that oil plays in all of our lives, and most of us didn't like what we saw.

Today, according to a recent Fredrick-Schneiders poll, "63% of Americans believe the U.S. can meet future energy demands through greater efficiency and without building new power plants of any type." Sixty-two percent of those polled indicated that the highest funding priority for U.S. energy should be efficiency and renewables. Despite this clear public desire for clean energy sources, efficiency and renewables continue to be afterthoughts—mere window dressing on a national energy policy that seems committed to propping up the past rather than charting the future.

One of the greatest myths surrounding clean energy is that it is not ready to do the job. As this book shows, renewables *are* ready—the technical barriers are almost entirely removed. The true barriers to energy reform are now, and always have been, political.

Over the past twelve years, during Republican administrations that espoused the virtures of the free market and a "level economic playing field," clean energy has consistently faced an uphill struggle. Current federal subsidies to the fossil and nuclear industries total over $50 billion annually, while energy efficiency, conservation, and all renewables combined garner just under $1 billion. During the Reagan-Bush years, funding for clean energy technologies was slashed by 90 percent. While it may have been "morning in America" for some, it was a long, cold night for proponents of clean energy.

Even against these odds, clean energy has made significant strides during the eighties. According to energy guru Amory Lovins, from 1979 to 1986 the United States produced fifteen times as much new energy from savings (efficiency) as from all net increases in supply from nuclear and fossil fuels and more new net supply from renewable than nonrenewable sources.

While the federal government has given over $100 billion in taxpayer-funded subsidies to nuclear power, renewables have quietly surpassed nukes in overall energy provided.

As you read this book and realize the enormous potential that these technologies offer, ask yourself if that potential is being realized. If the answer is no, don't simply throw up your hands—write your representatives and get involved in local struggles for clean energy. Clean energy is ready today—let's give the people the power.

—Steve Kretzmann, coordinator,
Greenpeace Global Warming Campaign

INTRODUCTION

The recent war in the Persian Gulf region drove home the point to Americans that their nation relies heavily on sources outside its control to meet its vital energy needs. During the Gulf conflict and for some time afterward, one could not avoid hearing about the nonrenewability of oil and the inability of the United States to control its oil supply. Likewise, no one could ignore the horrendous environmental disaster that occurred in the region from the uncontrolled burning of oil fields and from oil spills.

Such situations make many wonder about the current energy situation in this country. Why does the United States rely so heavily on sources beyond its control, which are nonrenewable and whose use greatly harms the environment?

Indeed, the way in which U.S. society produces and uses energy is responsible for its most significant environmental—and many of its political—problems. Acid rain, pollution, and the greenhouse effect are all a result of this dependence on fossil fuels. And because the majority of the world's fossil fuel reserves are located outside the borders of the United States, this nation must allocate a substantial portion of its budget to importing fossil fuels, rather than developing indigenous, renewable resources.

It is true that the current energy-supply situation leaves the United States politically, economically, and environmentally insecure. However, it is equally true that this country has the means to change all this. Renewable energy technologies, already in use around the globe, can provide safe, reliable, and economically attractive energy alternatives. These technologies offer literally lifesaving advantages over traditional energy resources. The various renewable alternatives are the subject of this book.

Renewable energy technologies currently supply nearly 10 percent of the total U.S. energy supply (and 13 percent of its electricity), and have the potential to supply much more. By very conservative estimates, renewable technologies could meet as much as 70 percent of America's current energy needs by the year 2030; many experts believe much more is possible. And a substantial portion of these energy needs can be met by renewable energy sources in a shorter time frame.

Numerous renewable energy alternatives are either available today or in some stage of development. These range from solar power, with which many are familiar, to less well-known sources such as biomass (the conversion of plant and animal matter into energy), wind power, wave power, and alternative automotive fuels.

This book discusses as the currently available technologies, as well as those being researched for future application. Chapters focus in turn on solar energy, wind power, hydropower, geothermal energy, biomass, and alternative automobile fuels. (Some observers tend to take the broadest view of solar energy, classifying wind power, hydropower, and biomass energy all as solar energies. Others prefer to limit a discussion of solar energy to the *direct* conversion of solar energy, treating the other indirect sources as separate issues. Here the second approach is used.) We will see how each technology works, what developmental stage it has reached, how it compares with conventional sources of energy such as fossil fuels and nuclear energy, its international applications, and its environmental impact.

Solar energy is multifaceted. Solar thermal technology concentrates the sun's rays on any number of receivers, which can heat a liquid and produce energy in the form of steam or electricity. In California, huge solar collectors provide utility-grade electricity for hundreds of thousands of homes at competitive rates. There are a variety of solar energy applications for buildings as well, ranging from passive design to water heating. Finally, perhaps the most exciting field of solar energy research is that of photovoltaics, in which solar cells convert sunlight directly into electricity.

Wind energy has been harnessed by human beings for centuries. Although older-style windmills still function worldwide to provide mechanical energy, the state-of-the-art technology revolves around huge wind turbines that create electricity. While California and Denmark currently lead the world in the generation of wind energy, many other nations are beginning to look seriously at this energy source. One percent of the electricity for California and Hawaii is now produced by wind turbines.

The possibilities for hydropower vary widely, both in the technologies used and in their various stages of development. Large dams through which water falls to help generate electricity, for example, are familiar to most of us. Some of the less well-known hydropower technologies include wave energy and tidal power, two methods of utilizing the limitless power of our seas. Finally, ocean thermal energy conversion (OTEC) is a technology that exploits the temperature differences between deep, cold water and comparatively warmer surface waters.

Geothermal energy can be tapped from a variety of potential sources within the earth. The only geothermal energy application in use today is the practice of capturing the hot water and steam trapped just beneath the earth's crust, but this hydrothermal source provides a substantial amount of energy worldwide. Hydrothermal energy is used in a variety of ways, from health spas at heated springs, to the provision of direct heat, to the generation of electricity. The Geysers geothermal field in California is one of the best-known sources of hydrothermal energy. Other potential technologies include harnessing the energy from magma deep within the earth's surface, from geopressured systems, and from hot dry rock.

Biomass energy is generated as simply as burning trees for heat, or by complex fermentation and thermochemical conversion methods. It is a particularly versatile energy source: it can produce energy in solid or liquid forms to replace fossil fuels, and it can also generate both electricity and direct heat.

Finally, alternative automobile fuels are an energy resource with which most people will probably have the most direct contact over the next several years. Gasoline alternatives and additives in the form of ethanol or methanol, or the use of compressed natural gas, are samples of the kinds of alternative fuels we will see in the years to come. Brazil and the United States are leaders in the development of alternative automobile fuels.

Where the environmental issues associated with each of these energy sources are discussed, I have attempted to be as thorough as possible, mentioning every possible environmental side effect. This approach may lead some readers to jump to the conclusion that these energy sources are harmful. But it must be remembered that virtually every energy source has some kind of environmental effect, and that renewable technologies are significantly more benign than the conventional technologies. The author has made every effort to point out any relevant environmental issues in order to be as objective as possible. Clearly, however, she places herself firmly in the camp of those who favor an immediate and substantial changeover to renewable energy technologies, instead of continued reliance on conventional sources such as fossil fuels and nuclear power.

Each individual renewable energy source offers some technologies that are fully developed and functioning in today's market. There are also those that still require some advances before they will be available on a widespread basis. For example, geothermal energy has four potential forms in which we can capture the earth's heat energy, but to date only hydrothermal technologies have been developed to the stage of commercialization. Likewise, hydropower can potentially take many forms, but not all of these are available on a widespread basis yet. Wave power, tidal power, and OTEC technologies are all in use in demonstration projects or in small-scale applications, but have yet to be used to their full potential.

It is not the purpose of this book to gloss over the problems associated with renewable energy technologies, nor to imply that they are all fully functioning and fully developed. In fact, an underlying message here is that it is very important to direct further development funds to these technologies so that they can fully develop their varied applications. Only then can they begin to realize their potential in providing environmental, political, and economic benefits.

As with any new endeavor, many of the renewable technologies still have room for improvement. Energy efficiency is often quite low as a technology is first developed, and then this improves with further research and time. The enormous progress occurring with photovoltaic technology is a case in point. Another important issue is the lifetime and reliability of the actual components in the energy system. Today's wind turbines, for example, are much improved over their earlier cousins and are now considered to be extremely reliable. Finally, the ability to produce on a large scale can come only with time. When a technology or a piece of equipment is new, it is not mass-produced and hence tends to be more costly and time-consuming to create. Again, great strides are being made in the photovoltaics industry, which can now create solar cells on a much larger scale then it could during its infancy.

Because every new technology must pass through a series of developmental stages, it is unrealistic to expect new technologies to compete immediately on an even footing with established ones. While many people criticize the renewable energy industries for not having made greater strides in recent years, it might be more fair to consider the amazing progress these industries have in fact made in the face of formidable barriers. These barriers are discussed in individual chapters in relation to the particular technologies, but here let us note the ones common to all renewable energy technologies.

Chief among the problems facing renewable energy development in the United States is simply that American administrations often have not been interested in such development. Funding for renewables was slashed successively and significantly from Ronald Reagan's first budget through President Bush's first budget.

The table on pages 6–7 demonstrates the decline in U.S. government funding for research and development (R&D) into renewable energy technologies.

Not only has our government shown little interest in renewable energy technologies but domestic business and industry haven't jumped on the bandwagon either. This is evidenced by the fact that approximately 65 percent of the sales from the U.S. renewable energy sector in 1990 were exports. Despite the immense resource base of renewable energy in this country, we are falling behind in the development of markets for our renewable technologies. We are actually increasing our imports and decreasing our exports of renewable energy equipment. This means that American developers of renewable energy are having to look outside their own country for buyers.

Other barriers to alternative energy development include financial inequities not directly related to funding, and infrastructural problems. Some of the financial inequities involve tax advantages for nonrenewable sources, which give these a distinct advantage in the marketplace over their renewable counterparts, and the granting of long-term financing contracts to fossil fuel and nuclear power projects—but not to those concerned with alternative energy.

Extraction industries, such as those drilling for oil and gas, are heavily subsidized by the government. These subsidies were not initially established to discriminate against competing energy sources, but rather to guarantee the continued expansion of the extractive industries. Unfortunately, however, the end result has been that today renewable energy industries have to compete in an unfair marketplace with these heavily subsidized industries.

Government subsidies for conventional energy technologies make these resources appear cheaper to the consumer at the point of sale, but offer no overall savings because the consumer is paying for the subsidies in other ways, such as taxes. In 1988, 91.3 percent of the U.S. Department of Energy's technology-specific outlays subsidized conventional technologies, leaving 3.3 percent for renewables and 5.4 percent for energy efficiency and conservation.

Infrastructural problems vary according to the technology. They may include the lack of access to transmission systems and the need for the development of energy storage facilities. Experts in the wind industry cite these infrastructural barriers as particular goals to overcome in order to expand their industry.

Some of these barriers seem to be placed intentionally in the way of the development of renewables. Established industries that feel the danger of competition from these newer technologies, and politicians who perhaps have supported the fossil fuel and nuclear industries in the past and are uncomfortable either admitting an error or simply changing

U.S. Department of Energy solar & renewable energy R&D appropriations FY 1981 through FY 1990

FY	Biofuels[a]	Wind	PV
'81	57.7[d]	83.7	153.2
'82	30.5	34.7	78.0
'83	21.0	31.4	58.0
'84	28.4	26.5	50.4
'85	31.0	29.1	57.0
'86	27.3	24.8	40.6
'87	24.0	16.7	40.4
'88	17.0	8.1	35.0
'89	13.0	8.1	35.5
'90[f]	15.0	8.3	35.1

a. Biofuels figures in early fiscal years are a total of the individual line-items for alcohol fuels and biomass. Although there were originally separate R&D programs for these energy sources, they were later combined.

b. Solar Buildings figures combine passive and active solar line-items in early fiscal years; these programs were later combined.

c. Total renewable budget does not include such other line-items as the Solar Energy Research Institute, Resource Assessment, Program Support, Program Direction, and fiscal year carryovers.

their minds, are two possible sources responsible for the uphill battle that renewables face.

As a result, the renewable energy industries have often had to fight against misinformation. The Safe Energy Communication Council (SECC) discusses some of the myths surrounding renewable energy: that renewables will not be available for decades, that renewable technologies are too expensive, and that renewables have limited applicability. None of these statements is in fact true. The SECC points out that many renewable technologies are available and reliable now while others are rapidly maturing, and that renewable energy technologies can compete economically with conventional sources and many are already in commercial operation. It also notes that renewable energy sources are in some ways more "practical" than fossil fuels or nuclear power, having great potential, wide applicability, and requiring comparatively short construction times.

There is no turning back now for renewable energy technologies. They have struggled against many technical and institutional barriers over the years and now find themselves firmly established as an important component of our overall energy supply. The key objective now is to encourage their development and significantly expand the percentage of our energy supply provided by these safer alternatives.

SOLAR BLDGS.[b]	SOLAR THERMAL	INT'L.	TOTAL[c]
74.9	119.9	12.0	501.4[e]
22.1	54.9	4.0	224.2
11.7	49.5	10.0	181.6
16.4	40.8	5.5	168.0
9.9	35.5	0.5	163.0
8.2	25.8	0.9	127.6
5.9	22.9	0.8	110.7
5.2	17.0	0.5	82.8
5.4	15.0	1.0	78.0
4.2	15.8	1.0	78.9

d. Numbers are expressed in millions of dollars. Budget line-items include operating expenses and capital equipment and are rounded off to the nearest decimal.

e. Regarding the $501.4 millions figure for FY '81: this figure includes approximately $220 million in various other programs which were not carried out in later years. This explains the larger difference between FY '81 and FY '82 than exists between other years.

f. March 1990.

(Adapted from and reprinted courtesy of Scott Sklar, "U.S. Biomass Industry Must Set the Record Straight," Biologue *[Sept. 1991], p. 3.)*

☐ WHY RENEWABLE ENERGY SOURCES?

If the reminder of the Gulf War alone was not enough reason, each chapter in this book points out the benefits of these renewable energy technologies over conventional resources. An important advantage to renewable energy technologies over nuclear energy, for example, is fast construction time. Renewable energy units can be built twice as quickly as nuclear power stations. Solar building technology can be installed within a month; photovoltaics take up to a year; and windpower might take as long as three years from beginning to completion of a project. Nuclear facilities, on the other hand, are estimated to take between seven and twelve years to come on stream.

Environmental issues are among the chief justifications for the use of renewable energy technologies. Urban smog, acid rain, the greenhouse effect, and the hazards of nuclear waste are literally threatening life on this planet. The organization Greenpeace points out that if current predictions are accurate and nothing is done to halt the environmental havoc we are causing, "the world will be unlike anything in human history." Some of the consequences are cited in the following excerpt from "The Greenhouse Effect," (pp. 2–3; reprinted with permission from Greenpeace):

■ the climate to which we are accustomed, and upon which we rely for food and housing, will change dramatically;

■ rainfall patterns across the globe could change, causing previously dry areas to be flooded and wet areas to become desert;

■ ocean currents and temperatures will change, affecting the basic ecological character of our oceans and consequently, worldwide climates;

■ fisheries, food production and agriculture will all be seriously disrupted;

■ plants and animal populations will find themselves in climatic conditions and environments to which they cannot adapt, causing the extinction of species to accelerate dramatically;

■ in the U.S. specifically, large areas of eastern and southern forests could be destroyed, making the midwestern grain belt a desert; up to 80 percent of our wetlands (which support our fish and bird life) could also be destroyed.

Economic and political issues also loom large. The hidden costs of conventional energy resources are mentioned often throughout this book. Likewise, the political implications of continuing to rely on foreign governments for U.S. energy supplies are clear. This nation cannot guarantee continued, reliable access to energy sources beyond its own borders. The renewable energy sources discussed here, however, are all available right inside the United States.

Whether or not the United States encourages their use, the further expansion and development of renewable energy sources will continue. The chance to be among the key developers of these technologies is already beginning to slip through our fingers as American companies ignore renewable energy developers and other nations pick up our technology. We will lose our ability to compete in a drastically changed international energy market if we do not quickly support our renewable energy developers.

Many renewable energy technologies are now cost-competitive with fossil fuel and nuclear sources, and some are even cheaper. For those that are not yet competitive, it must be said that simply because one energy source (particularly if it is renewable and relatively benign to the environment) might not be competitive today is certainly no reason to discontinue its development. If all inventions throughout history had to compete competitively from the outset with existing technologies, we might still be considering the wheel.

The costs of defending our access to energy located on foreign soil are excessively high and wholly unnecessary if renewable, domestic energy sources are developed. One report examining the costs of the Gulf War estimated the direct and indirect costs of that conflict to be anywhere between $164 million and $268 billion.

National security is a key issue for every country. Therefore it makes political sense to develop indigenous energy sources, which a nation can control itself, rather than relying on foreign governments for energy supply. Renewable energy sources are far more evenly spread around the world than are fossil fuels. The sun, the wind, plant and water resources are all accessible across the globe, with no one nation or region controlling a disproportionate supply. Fossil fuels are not as widely available, however: over 65 percent of the world's oil reserves are in the Persian Gulf, for example—as compared with 4 percent in North America.

The United States, in particular, is heavily endowed with renewable energy sources. In fact, it has been estimated that fully 92 percent of its accessible energy resource base is composed of renewable resources, as opposed to just under 8 percent represented by fossil fuels. One report prepared for the U.S. Department of Energy noted that "today it is technically possible for renewable energy to supply more than 250 times the amount of energy our nation uses each year."

The cost of guarding our access to foreign energy is just one of the many hidden costs associated with our current energy supply. One expert lists environmental costs, health costs, economic and employment effects, national security, and state and federal subsidies as extra costs that the consumer pays for energy today. When corrosion, crop losses, health impacts, radioactive waste, military expenditure, subsidies, and employment figures are all added together, the hidden costs of energy in the United States have been estimated to range between $100 and $250 billion each year.

While discussion of the applicability of renewable energy technologies often focuses on uses in the industrialized countries, these alternative energy sources will also play a vital role in the developing nations. Renewable systems based on solar, wind, hydro, and biomass energy are particularly applicable to rural communities that are not linked to national or regional utility systems and that have dispersed populations, as are often found in developing nations. Numerous specific examples throughout the book illustrate the practicality of renewable resources for rural areas. Reliability, affordability, increased independence and growth without increased environmental impact are all advantages to be gained for developing nations that opt for renewable energy development.

Renewable energy has applications around the globe. Industrialized and developing nations, rich and poor, regardless of political orientation or culture—all nations can benefit from a global transition to clean energy sources. The renewable technologies available vary tremendously, so every nation has indigenous sources of one kind or another available to it. We will now look at these energy sources one by one.

1

SOLAR ENERGY

When we look for alternative sources of energy, the most logical first place to look is above us, at the sun. The sun clearly represents the single largest energy resource we have to work with on earth. It is estimated that the total sunlight falling on the United States each year reaches 44,000 quads (1 quad = 1 quadrillion BTUs). To put this in perspective, the United States has consumed between eighty and ninety quads of energy in each of the last several years. So the sun's yearly potential energy represents approximately 500 times what we currently use. In temperate latitudes the sun's energy, when it hits the earth, represents one kilowatt per square meter of exposed surface. The solar technologies we have developed focus this light energy and magnify its strength tens of thousands of times.

Just as the potential energy we can draw from the sun is enormous, so are the potential uses of solar energy. Because of the wide variety of uses, any discussion of the practical applications of this energy can take a variety of paths. This chapter first looks at three important sources of renewable energy: solar energy as it relates to solar buildings, focused collectors for high-temperature conversion, and photovoltaics. Then it looks at energy storage, an essential issue when dealing with many solar technologies, and a few other, lesser-known applications of solar energy.

One of the strongest arguments in favor of solar energy (in addition to its being a huge, free energy source) is that it is significantly more environmentally benign than our traditional energy sources. As opposed to fossil fuels, for example, solar technology has hardly any harmful effect on the environment throughout the life of the solar energy systems, although the equipment used in solar technology is likely to have been manufactured using fossil fuels or other less environmentally benign sources, so the technology cannot be said to be 100 percent benign.

☐ HISTORY OF SOLAR POWER

Using the sun's energy is certainly not a new concept. Throughout history humankind has successfully harnessed the power of the sun for both convenience and comfort. The Greeks used the sun's heat for their homes and public baths by building large, south-facing windows which collected the heat, and massive walls and floors to then store it. Seventeenth-century Europeans used solar heating to protect imported tropical plants.

The modern solar energy era began to take off with the 1973 oil embargo. Public alarm at U.S. dependence on foreign nations for its energy needs led to increased research and development in the field of solar energy and other alternative, renewable, energy sources. In the past several decades solar energy technology has progressed through the experimentation stage and developed into an established industry offering the potential to provide the world with cheap, nonpolluting, renewable energy.

The differences between the state of the industry at the time of the oil embargo and today are staggering. In 1973, sales of photovoltaics were negligible, solar thermal steam plants did not exist, and manufacturers of solar water-heating systems were few and far between. Today the photovoltaics and the solar steam industries each represent sales of more than $200 million, and the United States has more than 350 megawatts of utility-grade solar-steam-to-electric plants.

Solar technologies are now close to or equal to other energy sources in terms of cost. Solar thermal steam-to-electricity is sold at approximately $0.08 per kilowatt hour, as compared with current peak-time electricity prices nationwide of approximately $0.085 per kilowatt hour. Likewise, photovoltaic energy values are now clearly the cheapest option for small, stand-alone electric generation systems. These are competitive with remote diesel-powered systems, and nearly competitive for certain specific utility operations. Solar water-heating systems pay for themselves in three to six years.

☐ SOLAR BUILDINGS

The U.S. Department of Energy estimates that we use about twenty-nine quads of energy (4.9 billion barrels of oil) each year in the United States to heat, cool, light, and ventilate buildings (36 percent of our total primary energy consumption)—at a cost of approximately $200 billion. Approximately 60 percent of this energy is used for residential buildings, and the other 40 percent goes for commercial uses (offices, stores, schools, and hospitals). Studies show, however, that the energy efficiency of such buildings could double by the year 2010, cutting carbon emissions in half and saving $100 billion a year.

Solar energy devices now exist that are capable of supplying all the energy needs of a residence, including electricity, water and space heating, and space cooling. But some of these devices are too expensive to be put into general use. The challenge for today's researchers is not so much to create the necessary technology, as it once was, but to make all of the technology economically competitive with traditional energy sources such as hydroelectric power and fossil fuels. Researchers are extremely optimistic that those solar energy devices that are not yet economically competitive can be so within the next decade or two.

The portion of the U.S. government's R&D budget that looks at solar energy uses for buildings was a mere $4.2 million in the 1990 fiscal year. (The total amount invested in renewable energy technologies that year was $78.9 million.) By comparison, research on nuclear energy was funded at $609 million in 1989.

The following sections summarize the solar technologies currently available for use in the home. Although there are only a few types of solar systems, each manufacturer offers a system that is unique in some way. It is clearly impossible to mention every solar system available today. The discussion focuses instead on the most common technologies.

□ WATER HEATING

Solar heating is one of the simplest uses of solar energy, and one of the most beneficial to the consumer, in terms of (traditional) energy saved and, consequently, of heating costs. The water heater is the most energy-intensive appliance in our homes: water heating accounts for about one-quarter of the energy bill in the typical single-family home. In 1990 consumers spent approximately $13 billion on energy for home water heating.

Water heating is currently the most popular application of solar collectors, and swimming pools and residences account for the largest markets in the United States. Commercial and industrial systems are becoming more common, too.

The principles behind solar water heating are very straightforward. The most important element in a solar water-heating system is the collector. As its name implies, the collector absorbs the sun's radiant energy and changes it into heat energy. A flat-plate collector, the type most widely used in the United States, is typically a large, rectangular box with dimensions ranging from two to four feet wide, four to twelve feet long, and four to eight inches thick. The collector consists of black absorbing plates with attached tubes through which a fluid flows to collect the heat. The fluid is usually water but can also be a nonfreezing liquid. The plates are made of a material with good conductive traits, such as copper or aluminum.

As each plate is heated from its exposure to sunlight, its heat is transferred to the liquid in the tubes. When hot water is needed in the house, the system draws the heated water in as necessary. The collector is usually located on the roof, or, if the angle/direction of the roof is inappropriate, on the ground nearby the building. Flat-plate collectors have been used in this country for 100 years.

Flat-plate collector systems are "active" water-heating systems. In these systems, a pump is used to circulate the water (or liquid) through the collectors. Cold water is drawn from the bottom of the tank and circulated. When the water has been heated, it returns to the storage tank, where it sits until it is used.

"Passive" water-heating systems are simpler and less expensive than active ones. These are cheaper and more reliable because there are no moving parts to break (or to pay for in the first place). A pump is not needed because of the design of the passive system. Here, the storage tank is placed slightly above the collector. The cold water (which sits at the bottom of the tank) descends into the collector, and when it has been heated it rises naturally and is returned to the top of the storage tank.

The Solar Energy Industries Association (SEIA) estimates that 1.2 million buildings, both residential and commercial, used active solar water-heating systems in the United States in 1990. Still, we are lagging behind many other countries in our use of solar water heating. Because of the relatively simple technology and low expense over the life of a system, solar water heating is being used more and more around the world.

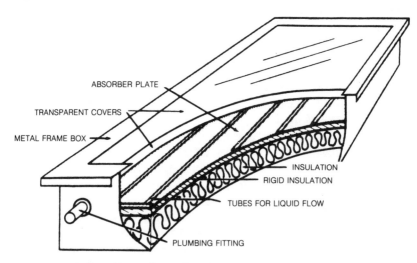

A flat-plate solar collector. (Reprinted with permission from the Conservation and Renewable Energy Inquiry and Referral Service [CAREIRS])

In 1988, 30 to 40 percent of homes in Barbados already had solar hot-water systems. Cyprus, Israel, and Jordan are other countries that rely heavily on solar water heating. In these countries solar panels heat between 25 and 65 percent of the water in homes. In Israel, specifically, more than 700,000 homes (65 percent of domestic water heating) have simple solar systems that cost less than $500 per family to install. Needing only $25 in supplemental electric heating per year, they pay for themselves in four years.

Flat-plate solar water heaters serve many purposes in developing nations, too. As nations develop, their need for hot water increases dramatically. Access to hot water can decrease the incidence of disease spread by contaminated food and water. Hospitals, clinics, and schools need hot water for cleaning, sterilization, food preparation, and laundry.

□ SPACE HEATING AND COOLING

Solar systems for domestic space heating and cooling are categorized as either active or passive. Both techniques are used in solar homes today in the United States and throughout the world. The use of solar space-heating and -cooling techniques instead of conventional energy can result in a dramatic decrease in a residential energy bill; roughly one-half of the residential energy use in the United States is for space heating and cooling.

Active Systems

Active space-heating systems are based on principles similar to those of solar water heaters. Here again, flat-plate collectors are commonly used. But active space systems must do more than simply heat water and store it in a tank. In this case, either air or liquid (water, antifreeze, or freon) flows through the tubes in the collector. If air is used, the heated air will be stored and then circulated through the house by electric fans and ducts (which can, of course, also be powered by solar energy; see the section of photovoltaics later in this chapter); if liquid is used, it is indeed stored again (as in the water-heating systems) and eventually distributed throughout the house via pumps and pipes.

There are three types of active solar space-cooling systems: absorption coolers, Rankine cycle coolers, and desiccant coolers. An absorption cooler uses the sun's energy instead of electricity, but otherwise works in the same fashion as a standard air conditioner (evaporating a refrigerant). A Rankine cycle cooler uses both a solar heat engine and an electric air conditioner. It vaporizes a liquid with a low boiling point with solar heat and uses the vapor to turn a turbine that powers a generator to produce electricity. The electricity is then used to drive the electric compressor of the air conditioner. The third system uses a desiccant (a drying agent such as calcium chloride) to dry the air by removing moisture. Water is then evaporated into the air to cool it, and then solar heat dries the desiccant. This process continues over and over.

Whereas solar water-heating systems are cost-competitive today, this is not always the case with active solar space-heating or -cooling systems, which still tend to be rather expensive. But research efforts are directed at lowering the cost and improving the efficiency of active solar systems. During the past decade in Sweden, for example, R&D efforts have succeeded in doubling collector efficiency while reducing costs by 50 percent. In this country it is generally expected that solar space-heating and -cooling systems will be cost-competitive within the next decade.

Passive Systems

The idea behind passive solar systems is that one can heat or cool a house without using any kind of "moving parts" (engines or other equipment) to do the work. The actual design of the house and its components capture the sun's energy and put it to optimum use. Passive heating systems use the windows, walls, and floors of a structure to collect and store energy. Passive cooling systems rely on the design of the house to remove heat and to prevent it from entering in the first place by taking advantage of natural cooling methods like natural ventilation and night-time cooling. Approximately 250,000 homes in the United States have been designed with passive solar features.

Research shows that passive designs are becoming more common in newly constructed homes. In 1988, 20 percent of all new homes in fast-growing sections of the United States such as Colorado and New Mexico were being constructed with passive solar design principles. These techniques are also appearing in countries as diverse as Botswana, Nepal, and several North African countries.

While passive systems are very popular because of their simplicity, they are not necessarily easy to retrofit in an existing home. (Owners who do renovate their homes can lower their utility bills by 10 to 40 percent, however.) The most effective passive systems are incorporated into a house during the design phase, taking into account such factors as shade, air currents, and the amount of sun entering from different directions at various times of year. When set up during construction of the house, passive solar systems can use only a fraction of the energy of a similar conventional building, while still providing a comfortable environment.

Heating
As mentioned above, these systems use the windows, walls, and floors of a building to absorb and store the sun's heat, which then travels naturally throughout the house. Such systems comprise five elements: a

collector, an absorber, a storage unit, a heat distribution system, and one or more heat control devices.

Large, south-facing windows collect the sun's radiation. Heat is then absorbed by and stored in a large, dark mass (a "thermal mass"), which can be a masonry wall or floor or even a water-filled container. When temperatures drop, the heat is naturally radiated throughout the structure into the cooler areas. (Heat travels naturally by means of conduction, convection, and radiation.) If this natural transference of heat proves to be insufficient, a "hybrid" system, using fans or ducts to aid the heat movement, can be employed instead. Heat control devices include heavy curtains to cover the windows, vents, and awnings. These devices serve to hold the heat in at nighttime and on cloudy days, and are an essential part of the passive solar-heating system.

Cooling

Within the home, many features can be designed specifically with cooling in mind. Windows can be placed to take advantage of breezes, attic vents can be installed, fans can help circulate air, and rooms and partitions can be designed to facilitate air flow.

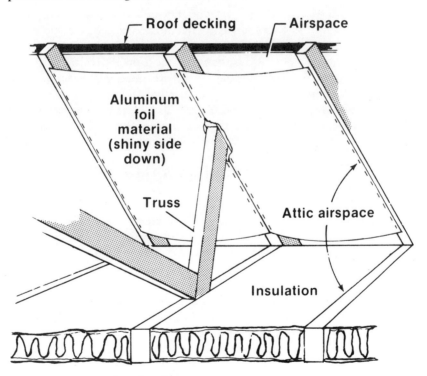

A radiant barrier. (Reprinted with permission from the Florida Solar Energy Center)

Radiant barriers in the attic are an excellent method of reducing the impact of the sun's heat on your home. An aluminum foil radiant barrier effectively blocks 95 percent of the radiated heat that would otherwise get through into the attic, and eventually into the house. (Note: this doesn't mean it saves 95 percent of your family's energy bill; it means it blocks 95 percent of the heat that comes in through the roof. Heat also accumulates in a home through walls, windows, body heat, and air infiltration. Savings are dependent on what percentage of your home's heat comes in through the roof.)

Radiant barriers are surprisingly simple devices. They consist of a layer of aluminum foil or a similar material placed to block radiant heat transfer between the roof and the attic insulation. They are typically attached, foil side down, to the top chord of the roof trusses or to the underside of the roof decking.

The costs for radiant barriers can vary widely, and as such are difficult to specify here. Basically, they involve simple materials that can be installed by either the homeowner or a professional. Prices will depend mainly on the type and quality of barrier material selected. The key is to choose a material with a very low emissivity— that is, a material that reflects the radiation striking it but does not radiate energy. Aluminum foil, for example, has a very low emissivity (0.05 on a possible scale of 0 to 1). It eliminates 95 percent of the radiant transfer potential.

Finally, the orientation of your house on the property is also important in terms of energy consumption. There are numerous ways to take advantage of nature to help reduce cooling bills. Using trees for shade, as well as placing the house along the axis that best protects it from the sun in the hot seasons, are effective techniques. Likewise, planting trees and shrubs to help direct air currents can help cut down on energy usage.

☐ ENVIRONMENTAL ISSUES

As mentioned briefly at the beginning of this chapter, solar energy technologies are considered much more environmentally friendly than are current mainstream energy sources, such as fossil fuels and nuclear energy. It must be remembered, however, that their production does have at least some environmental effect, as do all energy sources.

The production of solar collectors and other devices may involve the generation of pollutants during their manufacture, for example. Second, certain natural resources necessary for their operation, such as aluminum and copper, may be depleted if these solar devices enjoy widespread use. The fluids used in such systems, many of which are toxic, degrade over time and require changing, recycling, and proper disposal. Finally, considerable energy is expended in the fabrication of solar systems.

Even passive systems can be said to have some environmental impact.

For example, the use of cellulose in insulation will result in some depletion of wood resources. Likewise, some insulation techniques today involve the use of CFCs (chlorofluorocarbons), although substitute materials are being developed. All in all, however, solar energy technologies are still much preferable to their mainstream counterparts.

☐ FOCUSED COLLECTORS

With focused collectors (sometimes referred to as solar thermal electric technologies), we step up to a larger-scale use of solar power. These technologies can produce much higher temperatures and are therefore used in larger applications, such as directly for utilities, and to create steam and electricity for industrial purposes. Because of the wider range of use, and the target markets (utilities, industry), the market for focused collectors is significant. Industrial use of fossil fuels accounts for about one-quarter of U.S. energy consumption, and electric utilities account for an additional one-third. Clearly, the environmental benefits of replacing this energy consumption with renewable solar technologies could be significant. In 1990, solar thermal systems supplied approximately 200 megawatts of energy in the United States.

There are four basic types of focused collectors: parabolic troughs, parabolic dishes, central receivers, and solar ponds. The idea of a focused collector is similar to that of the solar heating used in domestic applications: these technologies use reflective surfaces to concentrate the sun's radiation and then use it to heat working fluids to generate electricity or to process heat. Solar thermal technologies have the advantage (over photovoltaics) of being able to store thermal energy in order to extend operation into cloudy or nondaylight hours by placing the heated fluid into insulated storage tanks. They can also produce steam for industrial processes.

The cost of energy from solar thermal electric technologies in the United States has come down significantly in the past decade: from $0.60 per kilowatt hour in 1980 to $0.08 to $0.12 per kilowatt hour in 1990. These are expected to drop even farther, to approximately $0.05 per kilowatt hour. In 1990 a plant in California was generating electricity at a cost of $0.08 per kilowatt hour, slightly higher than the cost of electricity from new coal plants ($0.06 per kilowatt hours), but a third less than the cost from new nuclear plants ($0.12 per kilowatt hour). It is projected that solar thermal technologies can be completely economically competitive by the mid- to late 1990s. Solar thermal technology is being developed and receiving more attention in many countries. Such international research is improving the cost-competitiveness, reliability, and efficiency of solar collectors.

Parabolic Troughs

Parabolic troughs are U-shaped mirrors that focus sunlight onto a linear receiver, typically a vacuum-enclosed glass or metal tube that runs along the focal point of the trough. The tubes are filled with oil or water that can reach temperatures of up to 750 degrees Fahrenheit. This kind of system usually tracks the sun on one, and sometimes two, axes.

The world's largest solar thermal power plants are located in California and are operated by Luz International. These parabolic troughs produce 354 megawatts of electric power, and additional plants have been planned that will produce an additional 320 megawatts by 1994. Luz International's collectors produce enough power for about 170,000 homes for as little as $0.08 per kilowatt hour. This cost is already competitive with peak time energy costs in southern California.

No gas emissions or waste are created by solar thermal plants (unless they are hybrid, in which case the natural gas, for example, does generate some carbon dioxide). The main environmental impact of solar thermal energy generation is in the land space used. The more recent Luz plants in southern California must use just under five acres for each megawatt produced. While this requirement may appear high, it is no higher than the land needed for other fuels (coal and nuclear) when primary fuel extraction and other uses of land are considered. Also, solar thermal plants use much less water than coal or nuclear plants do.

Solar thermal technologies have additional advantages over traditional methods of energy production. Construction times, for example, are significantly shorter. The first Luz solar thermal electric plants in southern California were constructed in nine months, as compared with a six-to twelve-year period for conventional central-station power plants.

Parabolic trough systems are modular and can be put together to produce large amounts of heated fluid. This fluid is then typically transported to a facility nearby to generate electricity. Their modular design also means that larger power stations can be created incrementally, as needed, with no inconvenience. The same can be said for parabolic dishes. Parabolic troughs represent the most mature solar thermal technology available today.

Parabolic Dishes

Parabolic dish collectors are also called "point focus" collectors. In this design the solar energy is concentrated onto a receiver located at the focal point in front of the dish. These collectors offer much higher concentration of the sun's energy and therefore produce the highest temperatures of all current concentrator collector technologies. (Temperatures of up to 4,000 degrees Fahrenheit have been achieved, although for most uses such high temperatures are not necessary.)

A parabolic trough. (Reprinted with permission from the Solar Energy Industries Association [SEIA] and Luz International)

The high temperatures achieved by this technology make it particularly desirable for generating electricity (for utilities) and in laboratories that conduct high-temperature research. For example, parabolic dish technology has been used in laboratory experiments to enhance chemical reactions and create expensive chemicals, to decompose toxic wastes such as dioxins and PCBs, and to decompose chemicals, such as trichloroethylene (TCE), that have contaminated the groundwater.

Because the computer-directed dish design allows the collector to focus directly on the sun's rays at all times, this type of system is highly efficient. Laboratory and prototype parabolic dishes have achieved efficiency levels of 31 percent.

Central Receivers

Parabolic systems are called distributed systems, as opposed to central receiver systems. A central receiver system uses many large mirrors, called heliostats, which focus the sun's light onto a receiver located high up on a tower. The receiver holds a heat-transfer fluid which circulates through it. The fluid can be heated to temperatures ranging from 1,000 to 2,700 degrees Fahrenheit. This kind of system also uses computer controls to track the sun constantly. The heat gathered from central

A parabolic dish. (Reprinted with permission from the National Renewable Energy Laboratory)

receivers can be used directly for industrial applications or to turn a turbine to generate electricity.

Solar Ponds

Solar ponds represent the simplest kind of focused collector. They are ponds of salty water that trap heat at the bottom, under three layers of water with varying degrees of salinity. Warm water will usually rise, but the layers in a pond block this action, trapping the hot water at the bottom with the salt, which makes it too dense to rise to the top and cool. The hot water is then either stored as heat or used to provide heat for other applications.

The unique nature of solar ponds in comparison with other solar collectors precludes their widespread use but also provides them with several advantages. In addition to the environmental benefits of any type of renewable energy source, solar ponds can be used together with desalination units to purify contaminated or mineral-impaired water. The pond itself can then become the receptacle for the waste products. A solar pond project in the late 1980s employed this procedure for the first time in the United States to desalt brackish water in a pond in El Paso, Texas.

Although ponds cannot have widespread application because they are very site-specific, several sites have nonetheless been established around the globe. Israel led the world in salt gradient pond research in 1958 and built the first small electricity-generating solar pond in 1979 on the shores of the Dead Sea. The pond supplied more than 200 kilowatts of peak-load electricity into the Israeli national power system. That nation's latest project produces up to five megawatts of electricity during peak periods at a cost of approximately $0.10 per kilowatt hour. Technological advances are expected to reduce that cost in the near future. Solar ponds are supplying power in other parts of the world, too. In Australia, a prototype pond near Alice Springs supplies up to twenty kilowatts of electricity intermittently. Plans for solar pond developments are under way in Mexico, Italy, Argentina, Japan, Portugal, Qatar, and Kuwait.

☐ PHOTOVOLTAICS

Solar energy can also be directly converted to electrical energy by solar (photovoltaic, or PV) cells. The term "photovoltaics" is derived from "photo" (light) and "voltaic" (producing an electric current). In recent years, photovoltaic technology has been capturing more public attention than all the other solar technologies. One reason for its appeal is that it can diffuse sunlight without concentration and can therefore be used in places that receive only moderate levels of sunlight. Thus, PV applications are not so geographically limited as solar collector systems.

The photovoltaic effect (that light falling on certain materials can produce electricity) was discovered in 1839 by a French scientist named Edmund Becquerel. But the technology was not developed until quite recently, after the production of the first modern photovoltaic cell in 1954. The development of PV technology in the last forty or so years gained a great deal from advances in solid state technology throughout the 1950s. Its development was also spurred on by the U.S. government's interest in creating a power source for space satellites.

The basic component of a PV system is the solar cell, which must be made of a semiconductor material. Although many materials might be used, the most common one is some kind of silicon. Silicon is used most often because of its abundance (it comprises more than one-fourth of the earth's crust). Solar cells are typically thin rectangular or circular wafers.

The workings of a solar cell are quite simple. When sunlight hits the surface of the cell, electrons are knocked loose from atoms, generating a flow of electrical current. Metal contacts on the top and bottom of the cell allow the current to flow through an external circuit to produce the electric power. The amount of electricity produced by a PV device

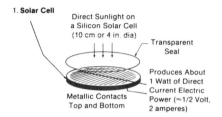

1. Solar Cell

Direct Sunlight on a Silicon Solar Cell (10 cm or 4 in. dia)

Transparent Seal

Produces About 1 Watt of Direct Current Electric Power (≈1/2 Volt, 2 amperes)

Metallic Contacts Top and Bottom

A solar cell. (Reprinted with permission from the National Renewable Energy Laboratory)

depends on the amount of sunlight it is exposed to and the efficiency of the device.

Solar cells are modular, meaning that many can be put together to form larger units, producing larger amounts of energy. Cells are wired together and mounted on a frame to form "modules." Modules, in turn, can be joined together to form "arrays." The electricity collected can be used directly on DC appliances (solar cells always create direct current, or DC, power) or stored in a battery for future use. It can easily be converted to AC power (alternating current, which is used in American homes).

The first solar cells used single-crystal silicon. These types of cells offer the highest efficiency of conversion from sunlight to electricity. Set in 1988, the current record for PV efficiency in a single-crystal solar cell, under normal light, is 22.8 percent. The drawback of single-crystal silicon cells, however, is their relatively high cost due to the fact that they must be comparatively thick. Polycrystalline silicon has a lower efficiency rate (15 to 17 percent in normal light) but is cheaper to produce.

The newest solar cells use amorphous (not crystalline) silicon and are referred to as "thin film" cells. This type of silicon absorbs sunlight well and can be extremely thin (one micron, or one-hundredth as thick as the crystalline models). It can also be attached to other materials, such as glass or metal, in a way amenable to mass production. The drawback, again, is a relatively low efficiency rate (7 to 12 percent in normal light).

In 1988, amorphous silicon accounted for 40 percent of the PV energy products sold worldwide. Though lower in efficiency than crystalline silicon, amorphous silicon cells form the cornerstone for solar-powered consumer products. Because consumer products typically need less energy than other applications, the lower efficiency of the amorphous cells is less important.

Other types of materials being developed for PV technology include gallium arsenide, copper indium diselenide, and cadmium telluride. Single-crystal gallium arsenide, for example, has demonstrated efficien-

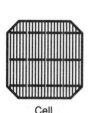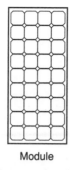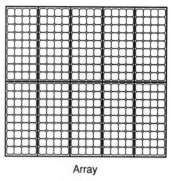

| Cell | Module | Array |

A solar cell, a module, and an array. (REPRINTED WITH PERMISSION FROM THE NATIONAL RENEWABLE ENERGY LABORATORY)

cies of 22.4 percent for thin films and 24.8 percent for conventional cells in laboratory testing. These are still in the developmental stages, however.

PV technology has many advantages over traditional energy sources. Among these are reliability (typical crystalline modules have a life expectancy of twenty years); ease of installation and maintenance; versatility (the modular design allows for larger or smaller energy needs); compatibility (the technology can work alone or in hybrid systems, with other energy sources as backup); and environmental friendliness (PV technology generates no fumes, liquids, or solid waste products and requires no water for operation; it does not contribute to greenhouse gases, acid rain, or air pollution; and it is silent).

It has been estimated, in fact, that 97 percent of the environmental risk of PV systems stems from the production of the energy system itself. This is because virtually no pollution is emitted by the PV cells during their lifetime. Silicon-based cells are more environmentally benign than the newer technologies, using gallium arsenide and cadmium-based cells, which contain minute quantities of toxic gases. Gallium arsenide, for example, is made using arsine, an extremely dangerous gas. (It should be noted, however, that these technologies are still considered to pose fewer environmental problems than conventional technologies.) Finally, land use requirements, as for solar thermal technologies, are less with PV systems than for coal and nuclear power generation.

The costs of a PV system in relation to "traditional" power sources depend greatly on the location and size of the project, and on whether there is existing power at the site. For example, one of the most economically viable uses of PV devices today is for locations away from the established energy grid. In these cases, the cost of extending the grid can be prohibitive, and PV installation is usually significantly cheaper.

The cost of energy from a PV system is high for the first year, but reduces to near zero once capital costs are paid because there are no fuel costs. The high initial cost is one of the reasons for PV's lack of market penetration so far, even though its competitive potential is significant. It shares this obstacle with many of the other renewable energy technologies discussed in this book.

Experts predict significant reduction in the costs over the next few years. There is some debate as to how low and how soon, however, depending on how much R&D funding is put toward the technology and how quickly efficiency levels can be raised. Nonetheless, experts believe that the cost of PV energy could drop to $0.12 per kilowatt hour by 1995, and as low as $0.04 per kilowatt hour by 2030.

At the present time, using photovoltaics to power individual homes is not quite cost-competitive in most areas—unless a particular house is being built away from the energy grid. But if one lives in an area that increases utility rates at peak times of the day (the average cost for electricity in the United States is between $0.04 and $0.20 per kilowatt hour; some areas charge up to $0.25 cents at peak times), PV energy costs may be competitive, or even cheaper.

The technology is perfectly applicable to homes, however. By placing solar cells on the roof of a house so that they receive good sunlight, they can power all the appliances inside the home. If more energy is generated than is needed, reverse meters can send the energy back to the utility, which then uses it to power other homes. Often, the homeowner will get a rebate for the power created but not used.

In general, the applications of PV technology fall into three categories: consumer products, stand-alone systems, and utility applications. Each of these is discussed below.

Consumer Products

Consumer products using PV technology have been on the market for many years and account for more than five megawatts per year. Many of us own electronic calculators or wristwatches powered by a solar cell, for example. Solar-powered battery chargers are becoming more common also. They plug into a car's cigarette lighter and provide supplementary power to the battery. The National Guard is among the biggest users of these solar-powered chargers.

A market has been developing slowly over the last several years for outdoor solar lighting systems. These systems are economically viable today; many pay for themselves within the first year. Consumers can now buy solar cell lights, which charge with the sun's light each day and then burn for several hours each night, keeping porches, walkways, and gardens lit and safe. Solar security lights (which come on when someone approaches) are very popular because they require no wiring and can be installed quickly and easily. The military also uses PV systems extensively to provide lighting in remote locations.

For consumer goods, PV technology is already cost-competitive in many instances. Small items, such as wristwatches and calculators, compete well in the marketplace. Other products, such as lighting systems, can pay for themselves in a relatively short time and so represent an economic purchase.

Stand-alone Systems

The largest market for PV applications today is in locations that are not served by a utility grid. In such locations, the cost of installing and using PV technology is usually significantly cheaper than extending grid power to the sites. PV technology is now being installed in remote areas all over the world and is being used for water pumping, lighting and power, power for vaccine refrigeration, and communications systems. One of the proven benefits of PV technology is that it maintains its reliability in any type of climate, from arid deserts to the frozen Arctic region or caustic coastal climates. It also provides a reliable supply of energy to isolated areas, which have had to rely in the past on sometimes irregular deliveries of diesel or propane fuels.

The U.S. Coast Guard has the largest number of stand-alone PV systems: 10,525 are used to power navigational aids. Each system saves taxpayers an estimated lifelong savings of $5,000 by removing the need to replace batteries at distant lighthouses and buoys. Many consumers may not be aware of the everyday applications of photovoltaic technology in this country. In California, for example, emergency highway telephones in some counties are now powered by solar cells. And in Florida, the Department of Transportation installed a solar electric system to light a highway sign that was off the nearest grid system. Hookup to the grid would have cost $65,000 to $75,000, whereas the PV system cost just $30,000. Utilities can find PV devices beneficial, too. Pacific Gas and Electric (PG&E) in California had more than 800 off-grid installations in place by the end of 1990.

Rural medical clinics throughout Central America have profited enormously from the introduction of PV power systems. Vaccine losses have been known to range from 20 to 50 percent in rural areas owing to unreliable deliveries of the fuel required to run the refrigerators. Solar electrics provide a reliable energy supply, thus guaranteeing the integrity of the vaccines.

The Bulape Hospital in Zaire was the world's first medical facility totally powered by solar eletricity. Here, twenty buildings are powered by PV modules, including an operating room that uses no back-up power system. Likewise, an archaeological dig in Belize, which was in an extremely remote location, benefited from the installation of PV modules. A 700-watt stand-alone system was installed which provided power for lights, computers, communications equipment, and a variety of other equipment.

Rural electrification projects have been spreading throughout developing nations. Great progress has occurred in the Dominican Republic and on the islands in French Polynesia and Greece, for example. Worldwide, more than 15,000 homes receive their electricity from PV modules.

In addition to systems already on-line, there are impressive projects in the planning stages. Five nations in the Sahel, in West Africa (Gambia, Guinea-Bissau, Mauritania, Senegal, and the Cape Verde Islands) have commissioned two German companies to establish solar water-pumping stations in their territories. The project will involve many decentralized solar systems to power irrigation pumps and other systems and will generate 640 kilowatts of electricity in total. The project is expected to involve construction of 410 pumping, 89 cooling, 303 lighting, and 33 battery-charging systems.

Utility Applications

By late 1991 more than thirty-five electric utility companies across the United States were using cost-effective PV systems for specific uses. While still reluctant to make PV energy a significant part of their energy base until they have completed further studies of its effectiveness, utilities are finding excellent uses for the technology. Some of these applications include mountaintop microwave repeater stations, transmission tower aircraft warning beacons, warning sirens, water temperature sensors, gas flow computers, street lighting and security lights, fans and lights in isolated rest areas, remote water pumping, and remote residences.

One utility in Colorado, K.C. Electric Association, has developed successful, cost-effective uses of PV technology in its system. This utility provides power to rural customers, and one of its biggest problems is the loss of power when winter storms damage power poles and lines. The main concern of its customers is to get water pumped to their livestock during these outages. PV systems have enabled K.C. Electric Association to set up water pumps that provide power supplies independent of the main grid, hence avoiding the danger of power outages due to winter storms. The utility is also looking into such experimental uses as PV stock tank deicers, which would keep water thawed for livestock throughout the winter months.

Basically, stand-alone systems still represent the most cost-effective use of PV modules, and utilities are taking advantage of this fact. While these remote uses of PV technology represent important advances, the solar electric industry believes that for the full development of the industry and the further reduction in cost to users of PV systems, it is necessary for utilities to accelerate their adoption of PV technology across the full spectrum of their energy needs. Industry associations are working with utilities to develop such widespread use.

The NEES and SDG&E Projects

Several utilities across the United States have installed research and demonstration projects that provide PV energy to private residences. Among these private companies are the New England Electric System (NEES) and San Diego Gas and Electric Company (SDG&E). These two projects, in parts of the country with very different weather patterns, are providing useful information on how PV electricity can function in varying degrees of daily sunlight.

NEES installed PV electricity to thirty-eight homes in Gardner, Massachusetts, and has studied the efficiency over a six-year period. The research has provided the company with a high degree of confidence in photovoltaics, both in terms of system reliability and in the interaction of the houses' individual PV systems with the distribution system.

On clear summer days, the PV systems on the Gardner homes were able to provide energy for twenty-five other homes without such systems. Customers there have seen reductions of about 50 percent in their electricity bills during the summer months. The fluctuations of PV power relative to cloud cover are still an issue, however. The NEES experience has shown that, in New England, days with total cloud cover result in PV production of about 5 percent of maximum capacity, on average. PV energy storage can alleviate these problems (see the following section).

Under good conditions, the NEES Gardner PV system produced about 270 kilowatt hours per month per house. During a three-year span, the typical annual energy production of these systems was 2,200 kilowatt hours. (It is important to note that the homes in this study are not aligned for optimum solar efficiency; most are oriented approximately south-southwest at 198 degrees plus or minus six degrees.)

In southern California, SDG&E interconnected a thirty-six-unit town home development in Laguna del Mar with rooftop PV collectors in 1986. One of the main incentives for SDG&E to study photovoltaics is that this utility is a summer-peaking utility; energy usage usually peaks on clear summer afternoons, which matches perfectly the style of PV power.

In this study, each rooftop had a one-kilowatt (DC) system, using twenty-seven single-crystal silicon modules and a high-frequency self-commutated inverter (to switch the power to AC). Typical peak output was 700 to 800 watts AC per system. Typical monthly energy production was around 120 kilowatt hours; about half that total went to each home, with the remaining half going to the company's grid.

Both residential application studies supplied important information to the PV industry. In each case the systems provided power reliably and safely. These studies allow researchers to look at such issues as the effect on PV systems of power outages due to lightning or other causes; the performance of the inverters and their effect on household appliances and the distribution system; and the system effects of fast and slow changes in sunlight, such as those caused by cloud movements.

The really important aspect of studies such as these is that they allow utilities to gain experience with PV and to prepare to use it in much larger applications, and they can do it gradually, without the enormous financial and technical risks associated with a full-scale, first-of-a-kind power plant.

The PVUSA Project

PVUSA, Photovoltaics for Utility-Scale Applications, is a national research project organized by Pacific Gas and Electric (PG&E) in California and also involving the U.S. Department of Energy, the California Energy Commission, the Electric Power Research Institute, and several other regional utilities. The research project is monitoring the development of PV technology for utility applications.

The project is studying, among other things, the efficiency of several different PV module technologies. Modules using arrays of crystalline silicon, amorphous silicon, polycrystalline silicon, and various thin film cells are being studied. The project is also studying larger arrays (200 to 400 kilowatts) with the aim of developing systems that can be adopted by utilities for operational service.

Research projects such as this are important because they represent joint efforts of government, industry, and renewable energy associations. Projects that focus on taking research and applying it directly to practical industry applications are essential, both for photovoltaics and for all the other renewable energy sources discussed here. Only in this way can we be assured of rapid development of the kind of technology actually needed by utilities and other potential customers.

☐ ENERGY STORAGE

The very nature of solar energy is that it is sporadic. Bright, sunny days produce vast quantities of usable power, cloudy days, less, and at nighttime there is no obtainable solar power. Likewise, the need for heat in buildings around the world often occurs just at the time of year when cloudy, overcast days are common. For solar energy to be useful on a constant basis, then, energy storage is often necessary.

Energy storage can benefit small and large power systems. Within individual residences and buildings, energy bills can be reduced drastically. For utilities there are significant advantages also. Energy storage allows a utility to separate energy supply from demand and also allows all power suppliers to make better use of solar energy, which is possibly our largest resource. Utilities that have efficient energy storage systems can realize significant economic savings and pass them on to the consumer. According to the U.S. Department of Energy, recent studies have shown that the nation's utilities could save more than $100 billion during the next twenty years by maximizing the use of energy storage systems to allow them to store for later use energy generated during off-peak hours.

Energy storage can optimize many of the systems discussed here and allow them to be used on a widespread basis, day in, day out, throughout the year. There are several ways to store solar energy for future use. Thermal storage involves heating masses of water or some dense material (rocks or bricks) and is an integral part of solar building designs. As noted earlier, the walls and floors of a building can also be designed to hold the sun's energy and release it when needed.

On a larger scale, massive underground storage can hold energy for months, allowing energy gathered in the summer months, for example, to be used throughout the winter. A technology referred to as central solar heating plants with seasonal storage (CSHPSS) has been shown in International Energy Agency (IEA) studies to supply up to 75 percent of heating energy needs, at competitive costs. Sweden has built several examples of this technology. This type of storage system is ideal for serving multiple buildings, such as in a district heating system.

Another method of storage is pumped hydroelectric storage (the transfer of water between low and high reservoirs). It is already in wide use. Other electrical storage systems, such as advanced batteries, superconducting magnets, and compressed air, are being researched.

In any discussion of solar energy and storage, it is important to remember that storage is not necessary for all applications, and that solar energy should not be considered only in tandem with storage. As we have seen, this energy source offers many applications for immediate energy uses. Also, it is often the case that demand for energy is compatible with solar energy supplies (the need for air-conditioning and refrigeration on hot days), in which case storage is not an issue.

The commercialization of solar power need not be hindered by any lack of fully developed storage mechanisms. Electric utilities typically maintain approximately 20 percent of peak capacity in reserve for shutdowns; the same reserve could easily back up solar power in the near term, until storage techniques are further developed. Hybrid systems are another solution. Hybrid plants in southern California use 75 percent solar energy and 25 percent natural gas and provide reliable peak power year-round.

Some experts believe that the amount of storage required for widespread use of solar energy could be surprisingly small. In California, for example, where demand peaks daily in the late afternoon and yearly in the summer (when the potential supply from solar—and wind—resources is greatest), it has been estimated that it is feasible to meet as much as half of the peak demand and one-third of the total electric energy with wind and solar sources with only a modest amount of storage.

Nevertheless, it is certain that storage can increase solar energy's role as a major energy source. Applications will include use in conjunction with baseload power plants to supplement their capacity and use with intermittent renewable power plants to serve loads during periods of resource intermittency. When solar power is being used consistently by utilities, in particular, as a standard source of their energy supply, then we will be making practical and widespread use of this free, environmentally benign energy source.

☐ OTHER USES OF SOLAR ENERGY

Additional uses of solar energy include desalination, detoxification, solar cooking, space applications, electric cars, and, in the future, solar hydrogen.

Desalination

Desalination was mentioned briefly in relation to solar ponds. In Texas solar ponds have been shown to desalt brackish water. Studies are also beginning in Florida, at the Florida Solar Energy Center (FSEC), to look at desalination as a practical solution to the lack of fresh water at one of Florida's parks.

While solar desalination had been researched in the 1970s, virtually no research on the technology has been done in the last fifteen years or so. FSEC intends to change that. Its motivation is that St. Lucie Inlet State Park, in Florida, is surrounded by saltwater and has no freshwater sources at all. In addition, FSEC is attempting to power the units using PV technology.

Preliminary studies, using commercially available solar stills, are producing about twenty-nine gallons per square foot per year under Florida insolation levels. The current barrier is cost: these simple solar stills produce water at about $35 to $46 per 1,000 gallons, which is cheaper than bottled water, but significantly more than what most people are used to paying (most people pay about $1 per 1,000 gallons for the water delivered to their homes).

The FSEC researchers believe that ultimately a technology called photovoltaic-powered reverse osmosis, or PV-RO, will be used at the park. While this technology requires significant amounts of energy, it has been used for twenty years in the Mideast and is being studied in some coastal areas of the United States.

Detoxification

Detoxification of hazardous waste is another promising application of solar technology. Thus far, laboratory research has been able to demonstrate the real possibility of this application for both contaminated water and chemical wastes. One of the advantages of solar detoxification is that the hazardous chemicals are broken down into harmless components and completely destroyed. Continued research into this field offers genuine hope for a safe solution to our growing hazardous waste problem.

Solar Cooking

Solar energy has already been proven as an efficient method of cooking food. While several commercially available solar ovens exist worldwide, solar cooking is still more or less a novelty application. It can, however, be practical in remote locations.

Three basic types of solar ovens exist: box, parabolic reflector, and multireflector. While the least expensive, box ovens cannot produce temperatures much above 275 or 300 degrees Fahrenheit. These ovens are insulated boxes with glass-covered openings that allow sunlight to enter and cook the food within. Parabolic reflector ovens reach higher temperatures than box ovens, which allows for a wider variety of cooking choices. Their drawback is that they must constantly be turned to face the sun. Finally, the most advanced solar ovens are multireflector ovens. They can achieve the highest temperatures and so can be used for many types of foods (including most meats).

Photovoltaics in Space

As mentioned earlier, the first real impetus to photovoltaic development in modern times was the U.S. government's desire to find energy sources for its space satellites. PV technology has played an important role in space exploration, and its development is closely linked to this field of study.

The first solar-cell array was used successfully on the Vanguard space satellite in 1958, with PV technology providing power for the satellite's radio. Solar-array applications in space have continued successfully since that time. Solar arrays are also being considered for use in the proposed U.S. space station. Here, PV technology could potentially provide power for space platforms, industrial processing applications, communications, and space-based radar.

Electric Cars

Solar energy can also have an important role to play in the further development of power for electric cars. While electric cars are available on the market today, there are still some significant hurdles to overcome before their use becomes widespread. Perhaps the largest of these is the need to recharge the battery quite frequently, a process which still takes a considerable amount of time. (Although new prototypes claim recharging times of as little as fifteen minutes, the norm is still anywhere from two to several hours.) It should be noted that the typical car is charged by hooking it up to an electrical outlet, so it is still using electricity produced from a standard power plant.

To use the sun's energy to charge a car, researchers have considered the possibility of solar-powered carports and parking garages. This technology is being developed by Southern California Edison and the South Coast Air Quality Management District. Here, PV panels on the roofs would provide enough energy to charge cars on sunny or cloudy days. This represents a clear step in the right direction for electric cars. Producing electricity for cars is more energy-efficient than producing it for refining petroleum, and hence less harmful to the environment (meaning that charging a car with electricity from a standard power plant is better than using gasoline), but certainly the best energy source is the sun.

An even bigger step in the right direction is the development of cars that are charged directly by the sun, with the use of photovoltaic cells on the actual automobiles. In this case the cells pass electricity directly into the car's motor and to rechargeable batteries on board. Such cars are still being used only in demonstration races, most notably the World Solar Challenge race in Australia. Still, advances in recent years have increased dramatically the efficiency of the solar cells used in these vehicles, while the manufacturing costs have decreased significantly. Today, many of the cars entered in the Australian race have efficiencies of better than 18 percent from silicon cells. The costs of a car with an efficiency of between 15 and 18 percent reportedly start at around $18,000. While these cars are not available yet on a widespread basis, their continued development is an exciting sign. The potential energy savings from their use is significant: the car that won the first Australian race, in 1987, crossed the continent on an amount of solar energy equivalent to what an automobile engine delivers from about five gallons of gasoline.

Solar Hydrogen

Solar hydrogen is a technology many years away from practical application, but it would provide renewable fuel in perhaps the least environmentally harmful manner of any energy technology known today. The technology needed—how to split water into hydrogen and oxygen by passing an electric current through it—has been known since the early nineteenth century. What has hindered its development has been the cost. Now, with the dramatic decrease in the cost of photovoltaic technology in recent years, hydrogen produced with PV electricity is a realistic proposal.

After the hydrogen from water has been separated, and then combined with air or pure oxygen, it releases its stored energy, creating ordinary steam as a by-product. Proponents of the concept of solar hydrogen believe that solar power can provide the heat and electricity necessary for the decomposition of the hydrogen and oxygen.

Using the sun's renewable energy to create a flexible energy source from water, another renewable, abundant source, is clearly an exciting prospect. The benefits of solar hydrogen are many. Hydrogen is an extremely clean-burning fuel. Solar hydrogen depletes no natural resources and poses no land-use problems. Furthermore, solar hydrogen is extremely versatile. In its gaseous form, hydrogen can be transported across pipelines; in its liquid form, in tankers. Solar hydrogen could serve either as a transportation fuel or as a fuel to drive generators and power plants. In fact, two prototype power plants have already been established in Saudi Arabia and Germany. Many researchers believe that solar hydrogen has the best potential of any of the renewable energy technologies currently known. Research is certain to continue into this energy source over the next years.

Clearly, the potential of solar energy in its various applications is enormous. The amount of energy we receive daily from the sun far outweighs our needs, and the development of a wide range of solar energy technologies promises a future in which the power of the sun plays an important role. The applications in current use, such as water heating, space heating and cooling, PV consumer products, and solar thermal technologies, all demonstrate how far solar energy research has already come.

2 WIND ENERGY

Winds can be created by a number of factors but are mainly the result of differences in air pressure created by the sun's heating of the earth and of the atmosphere, and surface heat. The regional differences in pressure that result from this uneven heating create wind. The direction of wind is then determined by topographical and rotational effects. Because wind is a continuously recurring part of nature, it represents an endless power source. It is also considered by many to be the most environmentally benign energy source available today.

Human beings have used the wind's energy for centuries, harnessing it to help grind grains, power ships, and pump water. Today's wind energy technology has developed significantly from simple farm mills of years past to modern electricity-generating turbines. An upsurge in wind energy research and application throughout the 1980s has resulted in a mature industry with proven, cost-effective products to market. In California, for example, where more than 75 percent of the world's wind energy is produced, wind power plants increased their output from six million kilowatt hours in 1982 to nearly three billion kilowatt hours by 1992. Costs also fell dramatically in the 1980s, to approximately one-quarter of 1980 levels, with the current levelized cost (cost fixed over a period of time, based on the forecasted value of both the energy and its cost, over time) of energy from wind generation in the range of $0.04 to $0.07 per kilowatt hour.

Today the wind industry considers this energy source to be not an alternative energy, but a viable, efficient, renewable resource. As proof, the industry cites that wind turbines currently generate as much electricity as that produced by a midsize nuclear reactor or a coal-fired power plant (and stresses the fact that the turbines can cost one-third less to operate, maintain, and fuel). Experts are confident that wind energy will play an important role in world energy production in the future.

☐ HISTORY OF WIND POWER

In early times the Chinese and Persians built simple windmills to harness the wind's energy and to help grind their corn and grains. Over the years, as invention and technology improved, wind power was used in such diverse applications as pumping water, powering sailing ships, and draining water from the low areas of northern Europe. Whatever the application, windmills have been a constant, from earliest times through today. Nineteenth-century windmills, both in the United States and Europe, produced only mechanical energy: they pumped water and ran mills.

It was only at the end of that century that experimentation with using wind power to create electricity began. Development of the technology was rapid, and throughout the first half of this century wind turbines were used widely in rural areas throughout the United States, northern Europe, and the world for the generation of electricity. It is estimated that between 1850 and 1970 more than six million small (less than one kilowatt) wind machines with mechanical and electrical output were installed in the United States alone. During 1973 and 1986 the wind turbine market in this country evolved from one that served agricultural and domestic customers with small machines to one that tied in to utilities and began using larger, more powerful machines (fifty to 600 kilowatts). An estimated 4,000 small turbines were installed between 1975 and 1980, although these were not always of the highest quality and reliability.

The wind energy industry has overcome many hurdles—technological, political, and social—to get to where it is today. Bad designs and hurried production in the early 1980s (resulting from the rush to get tax credits) gave the industry a bad name for a time. Current designs, however, have been tested and proven, removing any doubt about the quality of today's turbines.

Recent development has centered largely on California. According to Paul Gipe, a wind energy analyst, a special set of circumstances fostered interest in and financial support for the industry in that state. First, the National Energy Act, passed in 1978, opened the way for independent energy producers to sell their energy to utilities (through PURPA, the Public Utility Regulatory Policies Act, 1978) and also offered tax incentives to stimulate development. Long-term, fixed-price contracts offered by the utilities in the early 1980s also helped spur the growth of the industry. These contracts helped create the financial situation necessary to help the emerging industry. In addition to these national changes, California in particular offered a climate conducive to the development of wind energy. The resources (strong winds) and low-cost land were both available. Moreover, the regulatory climate in California was particularly favorable, and state tax credits were offered to supplement federal credits. Finally, a good number of wealthy individuals and a financial atmosphere that was open to investment in newer ideas were other important factors.

□ HOW MODERN WIND POWER WORKS

While there are many types of wind turbines in operation around the world today, these fall into two general categories, based on the orientation of the rotor axis. The two categories are horizontal axis turbines and vertical axis turbines. Both kinds of turbines can turn the wind's energy into mechanical movement or electricity.

Some newer turbines operate at variable speeds, with rotors that can be adjusted according to the wind speed, therefore allowing the turbine to work in varying wind conditions. Variable speed turbines are still relatively uncommon but are expected to be the technology of the future. (See the State-of-the-Art section later in this chapter.)

Turbines cannot work at any wind speed. Some cannot operate in slow winds, and most cannot work in winds above a certain speed, so they are shut down when wind conditions are inappropriate. This can be done manually, or automatically with some of the newer, computerized turbines.

Horizontal Axis Turbines (HAWTs)

The rotor axis of a HAWT is parallel to the ground. These turbines look like propellers; a typical farm windmill has a horizontal axis. Within this category there are still many varieties. These turbines can have one, two, or three blades, for example. Horizontal axis wind turbines are much more common than those with a vertical axis, accounting for approximately 93 percent of California's generating capacity.

With HAWTs, the rotors need to be kept perpendicular to the wind to operate as efficiently as possible. This rotation around the tower is referred to as the yaw axis. Maintaining the yaw axis can be done by a tail (on upwind units), by coning (on downwind units), or by a motor.

Vertical Axis Turbines (VAWTs)

With a vertical axis wind turbine, the rotor axis is roughly perpendicular to the ground. The most common type of VAWT is the Darrieus turbine, which looks like an eggbeater, but there is also another VAWT, the Savonius, which looks like a barrel. Vertical axis turbines can operate in winds from any direction. They also offer certain maintenance advantages, for the rotor and generator are at ground level. Although this type of turbine is much less common than the HAWT, both types are equally effective in terms of productivity.

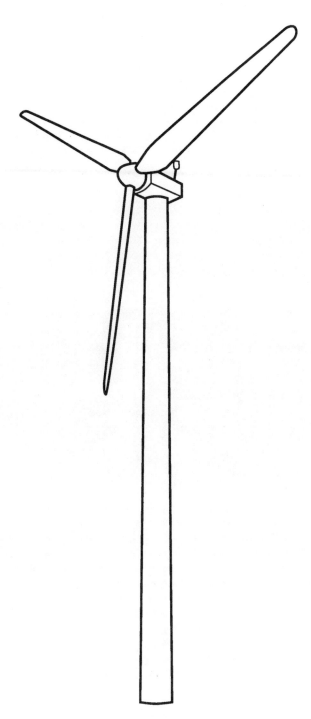

A horizontal axis wind turbine (HAWT).

DOWNWIND

UPWIND

wind

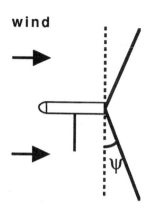

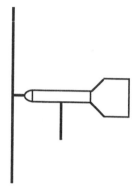

ψ, CONING ANGLE

Diagram of coning on downwind HAWT and tail on HAWT for yaw axis control. (Reprinted with permission from the Alternative Energy Institute, West Texas State University)

In addition to being classified by the orientation of the rotor axis, there are several other design variables that play a part in the workings of a wind turbine. These include the yaw, or the orientation of the rotor on the tower, and the positioning of the turbine (either upwind or downwind). A free yaw means that the machine freely rotates on the tower to track the direction of the wind. A driven yaw designates a turbine in which a motor actively adjusts the position of the turbine. Finally, a damped yaw slows down the rotation of the machine as the wind changes. Turbines can be positioned to face either upwind or downwind. If a rotor is positioned upwind, the blades rotate in front of the tower. A downwind rotor has the blades in back of the tower.

There are, of course, other working parts to a turbine in addition to the rotors. These are the hub, which holds the blades together; the power shaft, which transmits the rotational energy to a gear box; the gear box, containing the gears to produce mechanical energy; the generator, which converts the mechanical energy into electrical energy; and the tower, the structure on which all of the above are mounted.

Wind turbines are also classified by size, with three typical ranges. A small turbine produces up to 100 kilowatts; intermediate-sized machines can produce between 100 kilowatts and one megawatt; and large systems begin with a capability of one megawatt of power. Currently, small- and intermediate-size systems are the most commonly used; these can be found in any number of applications, from small units that help pump water for agricultural purposes to huge wind farms consisting of hundreds of turbines generating electricity that is sold to a utility.

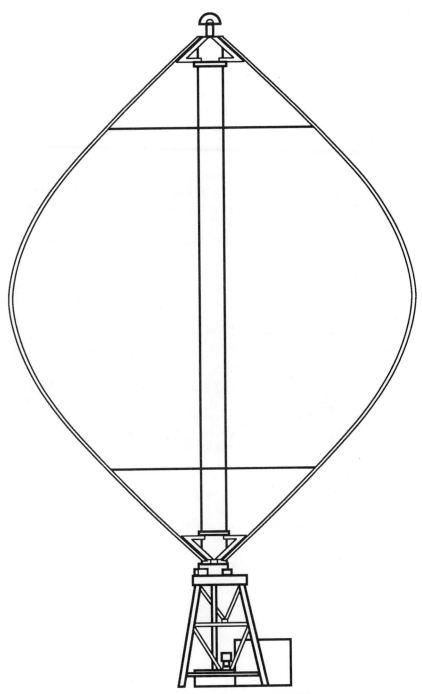

A vertical axis wind turbine (VAWT).

☐ APPLICATIONS

Wind turbines, whether in the United States or elsewhere, function in a variety of roles. They can be attached to a utility, working as a remote, stand-alone unit, operate as part of a hybrid system, or as part of a wind farm, or in any combination of these roles. Like solar energy, wind energy has traditionally served well in remote locations with no other available energy source. In these situations wind energy has provided energy at rates cheaper than could be obtained through traditional power sources, or with technology that could withstand weather conditions more reliably than traditional technology.

The water-pumping windmill, used extensively across the Great Plains during this country's development, is an excellent example. Today, small remote systems may also be used for battery charging, and larger systems, for agricultural uses, water pumping, marine navigation, pipeline telemetry, and to power remote homes. Wind-powered microwave repeaters operate reliably in conditions as diverse as those found in Oman or the Arctic Circle. One system in the Arctic was available to produce power 99 percent of the time during its first two years of operation.

Sometimes hybrid systems are used in remote locations. This is a combination system involving wind energy and another energy source, commonly diesel. In such situations, wind energy acts as a fuel-saving device and can significantly increase the power available to a remote location which be subject to irregular fuel deliveries. Or, simply, wind energy can offer a cost-effective combination to reduce the high costs of other fuels. For a hybrid system to work effectively, it must be designed to be compatible in size and production capability with the diesel system with which it will work.

The relatively new concept of wind power plants (also called wind farms, wind stations, or any number of other terms) reflects the development of wind energy over the past decade. Today utilities and private companies alike erect groups of wind turbines in one location to harness the wind energy collectively, thus creating a wind farm, or power plant. In California, there are several significant wind farms, each consisting of thousands of individual turbines spread across hillsides. One wind farm at the Altamont Pass, east of San Francisco, for example, accounts for nearly half of that state's wind energy production. That farm has more than 7,000 turbines, ranging in size from forty to 750 kilowatts, with rotor diameters as large as 149 feet. The Tehachapi Pass, also in California, is the world's most powerful wind resource area, however. Even though there are fewer turbines there, the Tehachapi wind plants represent more installed megawatts of wind power and produce more wind-generated electricity than the Altamont Pass.

Utilities are becoming more interested in wind energy production as the technology proves itself and more wind-generated power comes on line. Pacific Gas and Electric (PG&E), a major utility company in California, has become actively involved in wind energy projects in recent years. PG&E is working with the Electric Power Research Institute and U.S. Windpower, the world's largest producer of wind-generated electricity, on a five-year research project to develop prototypes of 300-kilowatt variable-speed turbines. Southern California Edison, another California utility, buys wind energy produced at wind farms in southern California for a portion of its supply.

Wind energy can be a significant addition to the power base of a utility company. Particularly when wind energy peaks at the same time as the utility's energy consumption does (as in California, where 80 percent of the wind-generated electricity is provided between May 1 and October 31, which coincides with the utilities' peak seasonal demand), this source can be a cost-effective help in providing service during periods of peak demand. Utilities can also take advantage of the power generated from remote wind power systems that are hooked up to the energy grid. In these situations, the excess power created by the turbine(s), but not needed for the particular purpose on site (agricultural, small residences, or industrial applications, for example), can be sent back down the lines to the utility to be used elsewhere.

☐ CURRENT STATUS

During 1990 worldwide wind generation reached a record 3,800 gigawatt hours. Turbines around the world provide commercial bulk power in California, Hawaii, Denmark, Germany, Spain, the Netherlands, and India, and numerous other countries use wind technology in varied applications. China has more than 25,000 turbines providing power for lighting and appliances in Inner Mongolia, for example. In Arunachal Pradesh, India, two ten-kilowatt wind turbines with a backup diesel generator provide electricity to a remote village and health clinic. Wind power is also used to pump water for irrigation in Egypt's desert area. These are just a few of the examples of the widespread use of this technology. More than 20,000 individual "utility-scale" turbines, averaging 100 kilowatts in size, are connected to the grid worldwide. The number of smaller turbines (of about ten kilowatts or less) is much higher. The United States alone has about 5,500 of these smaller turbines (of about ten kilowatts or less), with 4,500 of these connected to the grid.

Wind energy technology is in a position to make a significant contribution to worldwide energy supply over the next several years. Wind power is the least expensive of current alternative energy sources, and, although estimates vary widely, in the United States alone it is consid-

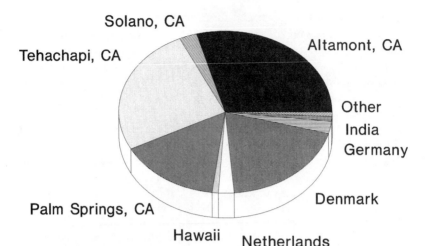

1991 world wind generation. (Reprinted with permission from Paul Gipe/American Wind Energy Association [AWEA])

ered to have the potential of providing between 10 and 20 percent of our domestic electrical supply. In fact, many believe that, among the renewable electricity-generating energy sources, wind energy is the most likely to provide a significant portion of our nation's electricity in the near term. The amount of wind energy theoretically available is estimated to be more than forty times our current annual energy consumption, but limitations in land availability and wind energy efficiency make it impractical to tap all of this energy.

California

California is currently the undisputed world leader in wind power, producing 75 percent of the world's wind generation. In 1991 it produced about 2.7 billion kilowatt hours of energy, enough electricity to meet the residential needs of about one million people—more than the population of San Francisco or Washington, D.C. This amount also represents approximately 1 percent of the state's electricity generation. Although 1 percent does not seem a large amount, it is worth remembering that California is home to one-ninth of the U.S. population and has the sixth largest economy in the world.

Most of the wind turbines in the United States are in three mountain passes in California: Altamont, San Gorgonio, and Tehachapi. These wind plants are privately owned and operated, and range in size from only a few wind turbines to several thousand. There are more than 15,000 wind turbines operating in California. Most of the wind energy produced in California is sold to two major utilities, Pacific Gas and Electric (PG&E) and Southern California Edison (SCE).

1. Solano County
2. Altamont Pass
3. Pacheco Pass
4. Tehachapi Pass
5. San Gorgonio Pass

Locations of California wind plants. (Reprinted with permission from Paul Gipe/American Wind Energy Association [AWEA])

The state's wind farms now produce:

- 1.2 percent of PG&E's estimated consumption, and at times provide 8 percent of PG&E's load

- 1.5 percent of SCE's estimated consumption

- as much electricity as that produced by California's oil-fired power plants.

Although California currently generates the most wind energy in the world, the annual installations of wind turbines in that state have dropped dramatically since the mid-1980s, when tax benefits, which had helped spur the industry on in the early 1980s, came to an end. In 1991, California was surpassed for the first time in the amount of installed energy: while only eighty megawatts was scheduled to be installed in California that year, Europe planned nearly 200 megawatts.

Denmark

Denmark is the world's second largest wind energy producer. Danish wind turbines generated 2.5 percent of that country's electrical consumption in 1991. By the end of that year, approximately 3,000 turbines were operating in Denmark, bringing the total Danish capacity to 400 megawatts.

Production of wind energy in Denmark has followed a rather different course than that in the United States. Whereas the aerospace industry has had a big hand in the development of wind energy in the United States (with groups like NASA and Boeing involved), the agricultural sector has been instrumental in wind energy's development in Denmark. This is largely because in the mid-1970s, just when interest was picking up in alternative energy, the market for farm equipment was waning, so the farm equipment manufacturers began to develop this new market.

In 1979 the first direct subsidies for the installation of wind turbines were put in place. This had the effect of bringing a significant number of new manufacturers into the industry. In 1982–83 development slowed because of a drop in world energy prices. Although energy prices have not increased again to the rates of the early 1970s, technological improvements that have dropped the price of wind turbines have spurred on growth. A real help to the growth of the Danish wind turbine industry has been the California market: by the end of 1990, approximately 7,200 Danish wind turbines had been sold in California.

The distribution and character of wind energy in Denmark is also different from the situation in the United States. In Denmark most turbines are installed individually and serve domestic, agricultural, or small-business needs. There are very few wind farms, and those that exist are smaller than typical American farms, with an average of ten to fifty turbines.

Elsewhere

Hawaii is another major wind-producing area. Currently approximately twenty-three megawatts of turbines generate commercial power there. The world's largest horizontal-axis wind turbine is located on Oahu, in Hawaii, and supplies power to 1,200 homes there. Other areas with growing interest in wind energy include Canada, northern Europe, and Scandinavia.

In Cap-Chat, Quebec, the largest vertical-axis turbine was constructed under the Canadian National Research Council's alternative energy program. The fastest-growing market for wind energy is Germany. Total installed capacity now exceeds fifty megawatts, and that country plans to install that much again every year for the next four years. Germany is expected to quickly rival Denmark as the largest domestic market outside California. Both the Netherlands and Sweden are also increasing their investment in wind energy. Dutch installed capacity had reached eighty megawatts by the end of 1991 and was expected to reach 100 megawatts by the end of 1992. The Swedish government has begun a five-year development program that is expected to install up to 125 megawatts. Finland is also seriously considering wind power as a potential energy source.

State-of-the-art

The reliability and efficiency of wind turbines are at an all-time high. Most turbines installed over the last five years are now available to generate electricity 95 percent of the time, generally shutting down only for periodic maintenance, which can be carried out at times of low winds. Today's best wind turbines have an overall efficiency rate (taking into account the efficiency of both the rotor and the generator) of about 35 percent. In other words, they can convert 35 percent of the wind's energy to mechanical energy. This exceeds the efficiency of many other new energy technologies and the 30 percent average thermal efficiency of conventional power plants.

The research and experience of the last several years have led to the development of several technological advances that ensure the place of wind energy in our future. All of these advances are available to manu-facturers today.

One of the most significant advances involves the development of new blades by the Solar Energy Research Institute (now renamed the National Renewable Energy Laboratory, or NREL) and several of its subcontrac-tors. These blades have the potential of slashing wind energy costs by as much as 20 percent. Testing has demonstrated an increase in wind energy output of 15 to 20 percent in winds ranging from ten to fifteen miles per hour when turbines are equipped with these new blades. The advantage of these new blades is that they have specially designed airfoils (the cross-sectional shapes that govern air flow around the blade). All former designs have used conventional aircraft airfoils, but these blades represent the first designed to meet the specific needs of horizontal-axis wind turbines. The newly designed airfoils allow the control of peak power, significantly decreasing occurrences of damaged blades and burned-out generators.

Variable-speed generators, mentioned earlier, represent an advance that may be able to significantly extend the life of a wind turbine. Sophisticated electronic controls allow the rotor to turn at its optimal speed in a wide range of wind conditions, thereby increasing wind energy capture. The rotor actually "stores" the energy from wind gusts and feeds it smoothly to the generator, thereby reducing stress on vital components and extending the life of the machine. Variable-speed systems increase the efficiency of a wind turbine by 5 to 15 percent.

The development of more sophisticated software to control the turbines is expected to increase operating efficiencies by another 3 to 5 percent. Dale Osborn, president of U.S. Windpower, believes that the variable-speed turbine, coupled with more sophisticated software, can at least double the potential utility market for wind energy.

Finally, the use of taller towers has been shown to increase the amount of energy captured. Studies have demonstrated that increasing tower heights from eighty feet to 160 feet, for example, increased wind capture by 18 percent, while turnkey system costs increased by only 4 percent. In the end it may be simply cheaper and easier to install wind turbines on taller towers regardless of whether they operate at variable speeds.

□ COSTS

The cost to produce wind-generated electricity has dropped dramatically in the last decade. Advances in technology, manufacturing on a larger scale, and increased experience have all played a part in helping to drop the cost of wind energy production.

The California Energy Commission (CEC) estimates that under current conditions and when operated by an investor-owned utility, wind power plants can generate electricity at $0.047 to $0.072 per kilowatt hour. The commission states that wind is one of the least costly sources of any new generating capacity available to the state, and that it has become competitive with coal and nuclear power. When compared with the costs of wind power energy a decade ago, this is a phenomenal decrease: in 1981 wind energy cost approximately $0.25 per kilowatt hour. The average price per installed kilowatt of intermediate-size wind turbines declined from between $1,300 and $2,000 in 1981 to between $950 and $1,100 in 1990. As a comparison, nuclear power plants being completed in the United States during the mid-1980s were significantly more expensive. For example, the 800-megawatt Shoreham plant on Long Island cost $4.2 billion ($5,200 per kilowatt), and Niagara Mohawk's 1,000-megawatt Nine Mile Point plant in New York cost $5.9 billion ($4,700 per kilowatt).

Operations and maintenance (O&M) costs of wind energy can also be quite low: O&M costs at operating wind farms range from $0.008 to $0.02 per kilowatt hour and average $0.012 per kilowatt hour. O&M and fuel costs of coal and nuclear plants were $0.022 and $0.02 per kilowatt hour, respectively.

The full range of costs involved in supplying energy from various sources should be considered when making cost comparisons. Decom-

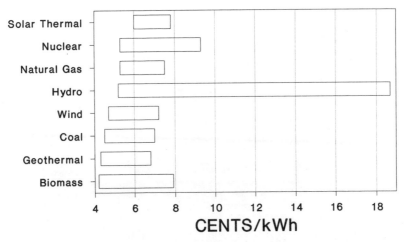

CENTS/kWh

Cost of new electricity generation, in constant 1987 dollars.
(Reprinted with permission from Paul Gipe/American
Wind Energy Association [AWEA])

missioning costs, for example, are an important factor. The cost of decommissioning nuclear plants has been estimated to range from about $0.3 billion to as much as $3 billion per 1,000-megawatt reactor in 1985. With wind energy, there is really no reason to ever abandon a site because there is no buildup of waste and the energy source is never depleted. However, some early turbines in the Tehachapi region of California were removed—for as little as $1,500 each.

Several other issues are important to keep in mind when considering the current costs of wind energy production. Randall Swisher of the American Wind Energy Association points out that today's prices are being achieved with relatively short-term financing of eight to ten years, at high interest rates. This naturally imposes a high debt burden in the first ten years of a project, and project rates could be much lower if long-term utility financing were available, such as is available for conventional energy projects.

The long-term costs of wind energy are important to consider, too. Remember that the actual fuel—the wind—is free. Hence, long-term use of wind power, as opposed to fossil fuels, can be guaranteed at a relatively steady price (necessarily taking inflation into account) and, perhaps more important, with steady delivery. In the long run, as supplies decrease, fossil fuel prices will inevitably increase. In such an atmosphere a free, renewable source like wind energy provides a more reliable, cost-effective alternative to traditional energy sources.

☐ BENEFITS AND CONCERNS

Wind energy technology, which exploits a renewable, domestic, environmentally benign energy source, offers many benefits. These range

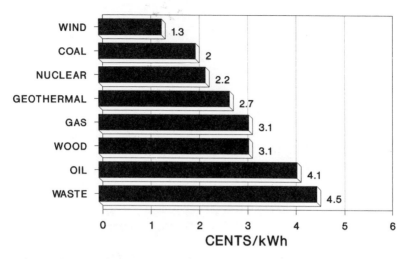

	CENTS/kWh
WIND	1.3
COAL	2
NUCLEAR	2.2
GEOTHERMAL	2.7
GAS	3.1
WOOD	3.1
OIL	4.1
WASTE	4.5

Operations, maintenance, and fuels costs, U.S. power generation in 1990. (Reprinted with permission from Paul Gipe/American Wind Energy Association [AWEA])

from economic and land-use advantages to utility and environmental benefits.

Wind energy technology provides more economic opportunity than any other energy technology, according to the American Wind Energy Association. Additionally, the Worldwatch Institute has estimated that wind energy creates five times more jobs per dollar invested than that from more conventional technologies. It has been shown in the previous section that the general costs associated with wind energy are also very competitive with those of many other energy sources.

In a 1988 study for the Commission of the European Communities, West German economist Olav Hohmeyer calculated that the societal cost of burning fossil fuels to generate electricity is about $0.03 to $0.07 per kilowatt hour; factors such as the depletion of nonrenewable resources, damage to the environment, and the cost of health-related services and structures are all taken into consideration in making this calculation. Conversely, Hohmeyer estimated that the use of wind energy provides a social benefit of about $0.04 per kilowatt hour of electricity produced.

Increased use of wind energy in the United States will provide the opportunity to reduce our country's dependence on fossil fuels. Not only will this reduce pollution from fossil fuel use, but it will cut down U.S. reliance on fuels from foreign nations.

Utilities that use wind energy gain flexibility in their power usage and planning. The modularity and simplicity of wind power generation allows utilities to develop increased energy supplies when needed, gradually. (Instead of building a complete power plant, they can add turbines

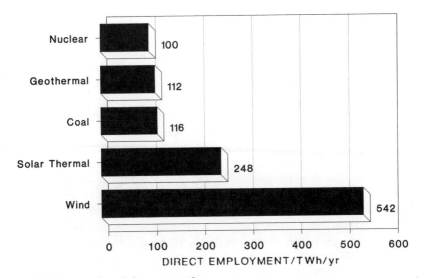

Jobs from electricity generation. (Reprinted with permission from Paul Gipe/American Wind Energy Association [AWEA])

as necessary.) The fact that turbines can be installed quickly and in varying increments also lessens the financial risk to a utility that chooses this energy source. Likewise, when a utility adds wind power as a source for its overall supply, it has a more dependable energy supply. Unlike solar energy, wind energy can be generated day or night.

Wind power has enabled remote parts of the world that had previously not had access to power to receive electricity. As mentioned earlier, locations that were either not on a grid or subject to irregular supplies of diesel or other fuels have been able to take advantage of wind energy.

☐ ENVIRONMENTAL ISSUES

Although the environmental benefits of wind energy, touched on earlier, make it among the most environmentally benign of our current options, it does have its detractors. Over the years, the complaints against wind turbines have included pollution, noise problems, danger to animals (particularly birds), electromagnetic interference (EMI), and excessive land use. While these complaints are often exaggerated, they certainly deserve mention here.

The visual factor is the most difficult to quantify because it is very subjective. Some people object strenuously to seeing wind turbines; others do not. Because most wind farms are sited away from residential areas, this issue can be avoided.

Noise levels, on the other hand, can be quantified. Although some wind farms in the past have been the target of noise-level complaints, modern turbines have solved much of this problem because they operate at substantially lower noise levels than their predecessors. Nonetheless, those living near proposed wind farm sites have voiced concerns about noise levels, and such concerns significantly slowed development of three major wind development areas of California. There are no standard restrictions in place, so the counties concerned set their own limits. To determine a noise-level restriction, typically the noise level is measured at a specified distance from the nearest property line zones for schools or residences.

Studies have demonstrated that the noise from modern turbines is, in fact, below that of normal street traffic. The accompanying table shows noise levels, in decibels, for different settings and machines (and the range of wind energy noise restrictions set by various counties):

Another concern, particularly on the part of some environmental groups, has been the deaths of birds that have collided with wind turbines. The California Energy Commission reported in 1989 that between November 1984 and April 1988 a total of 108 such deaths were documented in the Tehachapi and Altamont Pass areas. While one reporter points out that the collision of birds with similar structures such as bridges, buildings, and communication towers results in at least five million bird deaths annually in the United States, this is still a concern that the industry is trying to reduce by looking at ways to protect birds from the turbines.

Wind turbines with steel blades have been noted to cause some electromagnetic interference (EMI) in certain instances, disrupting television, radio, microwave, and nagivational systems. Because of these concerns, developers at new sites have been required to demonstrate that the turbines will not cause significant interference. This is not expected

DECIBEL COMPARISONS

Pain threshold	140	
Jet at 325 feet	125	
Rock concert	110	
Pneumatic drill	100	
Large truck	90	
Normal street traffic	83	
Ordinary office	65	
Normal conversation	60	Range of wind energy noise restrictions
Living room	40	
Library	35	
Hearing limit	0	

(Adapted from and reprinted with permission from "Noise," Windpower Monthly [August 1990, pp. 12–19.)

to be a serious impediment to wind turbine development, since most blades used today are fiberglass or wood laminate, which do not produce the same effect, and since the problem of interference is not widespread. For example, workers at many wind farms use radios to communicate, and report minimal interference.

Finally, the issue of land use is often discussed with the development of wind farms—these facilities have been criticized for using up too much land. Field experience in the United States indicates that most projects occupy fewer than twenty acres per megawatt, however. It is important to note, when discussing the land used by wind farms, that very little of the land is actually taken up; the technology lends itself perfectly to cohabitation with other activities. In California the land is used also for grazing, and in fact land values went up quite significantly—from $400 to $2,000 per acre—when the wind farms were installed. In Europe, where land is at a premium, the land surrounding wind farms is used for agriculture; crops are planted right up to the base of the towers. One expert has noted that wind farms would also lend themselves well to cohabitation with other alterntive energy forms, such as solar thermal and photovoltaics.

Land disturbance caused by the erection of wind turbines is also minimal. The figures above refer to land actually used, but of that land, only a small percentage is in fact disturbed. A study of two projects on steep terrain in California (steep terrain projects generally disturb more land area) revealed that the soil from 7 to 10 percent of the total project area was disturbed for road and pad construction. And some of the land lease agreements between landowners and wind plant operators stipulate the maximum amount of land that can be removed from grazing. In at least one case the lease limits permanent disturbance to no more than 5 percent of the land. Wind farms have proven themselves able to function within these limits.

As with many other renewable sources, much of the environmental benefit to be had from wind energy lies in what it does not do. The generation of wind power creates no air or water pollution, and its use helps alleviate current environmental problems by displacing energy produced by conventional, polluting methods. For example, the wind energy created in California in one year displaces the energy equivalent of 3.8 million barrels of oil and avoids about 2.7 billion pounds of carbon emissions. It also avoids fifteen million pounds of pollutants such as sulfur oxides (SO_x) and nitrogen oxides (NO_x), which contribute to smog and acid rain. It would take a forest of between 100 and 200 million trees to provide the same benefit to air quality.

□ THE FUTURE

When federal tax credits for the development of wind energy ran out in 1985, many expected the demise of the industry, but this has not come to pass. Several companies have survived and are now members of a stable industry with a solid future. Despite the loss of tax credits, technological advances that have brought down the cost of wind turbines have ensured the continuation of wind turbine installations. In fact, nearly half of today's wind-generating capacity in California has been installed without federal energy tax credits.

In a very encouraging breakthrough in 1991, the American Wind Energy Association managed to make some headway in increasing this country's R&D budget for wind energy. The association's efforts resulted in Congress nearly doubling the annual DOE budget for wind power research—to $21.4 million. (It must be noted, however, that despite these increases, the amount of R&D funding for wind, and other renewable energy technologies, is negligible as compared with that for fossil fuels and nuclear energy.) The group is also lobbying for a production incentive of $0.025 per kilowatt hour, but this will take several years to achieve, if it can be achieved at all.

Perhaps most important, the utilities believe in the future of wind power. By the end of the 1990s, PG&E expects wind technology to become the "most economic new source" of electricity. The California Energy Commission also sees wind energy as an important future energy source: that group's fuel diversity policy proposes that wind energy provide 10 percent of the state's electrical supply by the year 2000.

The choices of areas for future development of wind energy in this country are almost limitless. Studies have already been done that show enormous potential for wind energy in many locations around the United States. California, although it has been the most developed site so far, does not in fact offer the best wind resources available in this country. About 90 percent of the wind power potential in the United States is in twelve contiguous states across the middle of the country. There are actually sixteen states with potential equal to or greater than that of California. In order of greatest potential, these are North Dakota, Texas, Kansas, Montana and South Dakota (tied), Nebraska, Wyoming, Oklahoma, Minnesota, Iowa, Colorado, New Mexico, Idaho, New York, Illinois, and Michigan. These states are not the only ones with wind potential, however. The U.S. Department of Energy has conducted studies that indicate sufficient resources for utility-grade wind energy in thirty-seven states.

Unlike California, the area of the country encompassing the sixteen states with the best wind energy potential is served by low-cost, coal-fired plants and federally subsidized hydroelectric stations, so the immediate need for alternative sources is not so obvious. Many believe that for this Great Plains area to be developed, the challenge rests in establishing mechanisms for "wheeling" (transferring the energy across power lines) the wind energy from the area to other parts of the country. In fact, experts agree that the massive deployment of wind energy in the United States may not happen without additional electrical transmission facilities and other infrastructure required to deliver the electricity where and when it is needed.

Randall Swisher of the American Wind Energy Association has stated that a realistic goal for U.S. energy policy is for wind energy to provide 20 percent of U.S. electric capacity within the next three decades. To reach this goal, several steps must be taken: reasonable financial contracts must be made available for wind energy projects; information needs to be disseminated to policymakers at both the state and federal levels on the progress and potential of wind energy; and regulatory reform should be instituted. The regulatory system in place today is geared toward conventional energy sources, and as such, is weighed against wind and other renewable energy sources. For example, no adjustments are currently made in overall cost comparisons in recognition of the clean energy premium provided by wind (and other) energy in comparison to fossil fuels. The German study mentioned earlier, which takes into account the social and environmental benefits of cleaner, safer energy sources, addresses this issue. Widespread adoption of policies that consider the full-cycle costs of energy sources is critical.

There is no question that wind energy will be developed in the United States and contribute further to the overall global energy supply. Development of wind energy promises to continue in other countries as well. Denmark, the Netherlands, the United Kingdom, Italy, Spain, and India all have more ambitious wind energy technology programs than does the United States. A particularly encouraging sign is that France, a country which has long prided itself on its nuclear industry, is relaunching a small wind energy program. In an interesting development, Denmark has begun development of a wind farm off its coast—the first wind energy plant to be developed offshore. The location offers an opportunity to take advantage of strong sea winds while avoiding complaints of noise and visual disturbances. The offshore wind farm is expected to generate twelve million kilowatt hours of electricity each year when it comes into operation, provided by eleven 450 kilowatt turbines. The potential for wind energy generation around the globe is enormous. It has been estimated that it could provide many countries with one-fifth or more of their electricity. Northern Europe, northern Africa, and South America are among the areas with the greatest potential.

As both international and domestic experience with wind energy continues, the costs and efficiency of wind energy will improve even more. For example, the U.S. Department of Energy and industry analysts project that during the next twenty years the costs of wind electricity at sites with moderate wind resources could fall to $0.035 per kilowatt hour. Sites with stronger winds could be even cheaper. In short: wind energy technologies have proven themselves efficient, reliable, and cost-effective. It remains only for governments and industry to develop them to their full potential.

3

HYDROPOWER

There are several ways of tapping the energy in flowing water, ranging from huge hydroelectric power plants to systems that can exploit both tidal power and wave power. A newer interest has also developed in ocean thermal energy conversion, exploiting the difference in temperature between the sea depths and the surface waters. Only a few commercial or demonstration facilities have been developed to harness the power of the oceans through tides, waves, or temperature difference between surface and deep waters; most facilities working in these areas are experimental at this time. On the other hand, hydroelectric power through dams or run-of-river systems has been used for years.

□ HYDROELECTRIC POWER

Hydropower is considered by many to be a form of solar energy, because the sun actually takes water from the earth through evaporation. The water then returns to the earth when it rains, filling rivers and streams which eventually flow into the oceans. It is the flowing water in the rivers and streams that is used for conventional hydroelectric power generation.

The idea behind hydroelectric power is quite straightforward: it harnesses the kinetic energy of falling water. Falling water, which has been stored behind a dam or else flows naturally along a river, passes through a turbine, which turns a generator and produces electricity. The falling water can, of course, also produce mechanical energy, as in the case of water mills, which were used (and still are) for grinding grain.

Hydroelectricity is the oldest form of electric generation used today. It is generally considered the most reliable as well, although drought years can clearly affect its supply. The summer drought of 1988, for example, caused a reduction in U.S. hydropower production by 25 percent. In the United States, conventional hydropower accounted for the largest share of electric capacity (71,533 megawatts) provided by renewable energy sources in 1991. It regularly supplies 10 to 14 percent of the nation's electric energy each year. On a global scale, hydropower sources provide more than one-quarter of the world's electricity.

The History of Hydroelectric Power

Although the energy from falling water has been used for centuries for mechanical power, hydroelectric systems did not appear in the United States until the mid-1800s, and these were relatively small. The first major plant was completed at Niagara Falls in 1878. By the 1930s hydropower was providing 40 percent of the total electric energy generated in this country. (At that time the construction of major dams was taking place in other countries, too, including Russia and India.) Over the years, other energy sources have become more prevalent, and the percentage of electric power provided by hydroelectric sources has slowly decreased. In 1965 this amount had decreased to approximately 20 percent, and this downward trend has continued to the present.

Through the 1970s, hydro systems around the world were commonly large-scale dams used to supply the national grid. This trend has changed over the past several decades, and today new hydroelectric projects are typically smaller systems. Some of the reasons for this change are the ever-decreasing number of suitable sites for major dams and both environmental and economic concerns.

The Technology

Hydroelectric systems are defined both by their size and by the way they use the water's power. Large hydroelectric plants are usually considered to be those that can generate more than thirty megawatts, whereas small systems produce less than thirty megawatts. (Some experts further divide plants into micro-hydro systems, but for convenience this text will only differentiate between small and large facilities.)

The majority of hydroelectric systems use a dam or some other structure to capture and store water, which will eventually be released through a turbine. A less common method is to place turbines in pipes in the middle of a river's stream, therefore avoiding the need to block the water flow. Because of these systems' lessened environmental impact and lower construction costs, such run-of-river devices are increasing in popularity. Large hydro facilities are invariably dams, whereas smaller systems may use either a dam or a flow-through system. Finally, a third type of hydroelectric power generation is the pumped storage method, in which water is pumped during off-peak times to a higher reservoir for use in peak hours.

Two factors that determine the amount of energy a hydroelectric system can create are the head and flow of the water. The head is the

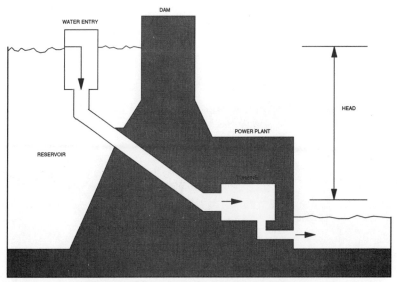

Dam layout. (Reprinted with permission from the California Public Utilities Commission)

height of the falling water from the point at which it begins its descent to the lowest point, below the turbine. The flow is the speed at which the water passes through the system. While various combinations of head and flow can be used, a facility that has a high head and a low flow is more economical than a system with a high flow and low head.

With a large facility using a dam or other structure, the water is blocked and stored until it is needed. Then the water is released through penstocks, large pipes that direct the water to the turbine in the power plant. The turbine is connected to a generator, which turns because of the power of the flowing water and produces electricity. Transmission lines then send the power from the power plant to the electrical distribution system.

Run-of-river facilities place the pipes directly in the flow of a stream, with turbines in the pipes. This allows some of the river to continue flowing naturally while the facility can capture energy from the water that passes through the turbines in the pipes.

Pumped storage is a method of reusing the water that has passed through the turbine and storing it for later use, when it is most cost-effective, or in emergencies. The water is pumped through a reversible turbine from a lower to a higher reservoir. Pumped storage systems actually use more energy than they produce, but they are still useful to a facility because they can operate at times when electricity is most costly to produce. (The pumping is done during off-peak hours, when the energy is at its cheapest.)

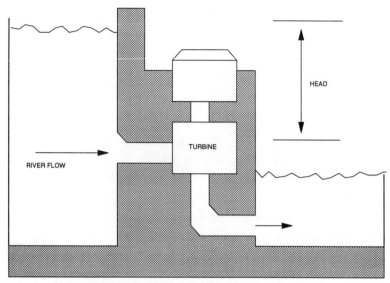

Run-of-river layout. (Reprinted with permission from the California Public Utilities Commission)

Current Status

As mentioned earlier, hydroelectric facilities supply anywhere from 10 to 14 percent of the U.S. electricity supply. The average annual energy supplied by current hydroelectric capacity is 302 billion kilowatt hours, or about 3.08 quads.

Worldwide, hydroelectric facilities provide approximately 25 percent of the electricity supply. Hydropower plants operate in eighty-six countries. One researcher has stated that in the last forty years the amount of water trapped behind large dams has increased twenty-five-fold and now amounts to approximately 5,000 cubic kilometers. He further notes that all artificial reservoirs now hold approximately 13 percent of all worldwide runoff of rivers to the oceans.

Some of the largest dams are the Hoover Dam (1,455 megawatts) and the Grand Coulee Dam (6,180 megawatts) in the United States and the Guri Dam (10,000 megawatts) in Venezuela. India has built more large dams than any other nation. The Columbia River hydroelectric network, which consists of nineteen major dams (including the Grand Coulee) and more than 100 additional multipurpose dams, is the world's largest hydroelectric power system. The entire system is capable of producing an average of 12,000 megawatts.

The main application of hydropower energy is in the bulk power market, for federal and state agencies, cities and utilities, for example. Hydropower is indispensable for these users because of its ability to provide power on demand: a hydroelectric facility can produce energy in seconds, something which fossil fuel and nuclear facilities cannot do.

Most major sources of large hydroelectric power in industrial nations have already been exploited. Those that have not tend to have been designated as protected areas. These nations are now looking at retrofitting existing dams to get more energy from them, or at constructing smaller facilities. Lesser-developed countries are building both small and larger facilities.

Future Potential

While hydroelectric power will certainly remain an important factor in the U.S. energy profile for some time, opinion is divided as to how much more significant development of this energy source will take place. Environmental concerns, and the fact that most sites for major dams either have been used or have been protected, are key reasons for this uncertainty. Nevertheless, retrofitting and upgrading of existing facilities is still likely to take place.

The actual undeveloped capacity throughout the country is significant, however, whether it is eventually developed or not. The Federal Energy Regulatory Commission (FERC) estimated that in 1988 the undeveloped hydropower capacity, not including that excluded from development by the National Wild and Scenic River Act of 1968, was 95.2 gigawatts (consisting of 76.1 gigawatts of conventional and 19.1 gigawatts of pumped storage). However, 70 percent of this was to be uneconomical to develop. Assuming no change in the situation, an Interlaboratory White Paper on renewable energy produced by several of the national research laboratories projects that only thirteen gigawatts (eight gigawatts of conventional and five gigawatts of pumped storage) will be developed by 2030.

Another reason for the estimated overall cutback in hydropower's contribution to worldwide energy is the fact that many large projects are having problems with silt buildup. These problems do not seem to have been solved over the many years of experience with this dilemma: a study done for the World Bank in 1988 led researchers to estimate that about 1 percent of the world's reservoir storage capacity is consumed by silt every year.

In the developing nations there still exists significant potential for hydropower facilities, and it seems far more likely that sites will be developed in these countries than in the developed nations, for the reasons stated above. The U.S. Agency for International Development (U.S. AID) estimates that the potential for hydroelectric development around the globe includes 711,900 megawatts in Asia and the Middle East, 550,000 megawatts in Latin America, 308,000 megawatts in Africa, and 39,000 megawatts in Oceania. Both large and small facilities continue to be developed throughout the world, but here too the trend seems to be away from large projects.

The United States, with an ever-decreasing number of sites available for development, has shifted its development strategy to one of upgrading and retrofitting existing facilities to increase hydroelectric production. It has been estimated that 15,300 megawatts of capacity could be added this way. Upgrading existing dams involves replacing older turbines with more efficient ones and bringing back on-line dams, which were previously abandoned or dismantled in the 1950s and 1960s when fossil fuel prices were cheaper. According to the FERC, refurbishing these retired sites, most of which are small, would require only minor work. Also, many existing dams have no electric-generating facilities. These are typically dams used for flood control, water supply reservoirs, or navigation dams—sites which could be retrofitted to allow them to generate power. The U.S. Department of Energy estimated in 1990 that there were 2,600 such dams at which conventional hydropower could be developed.

The problem of relicensing may also play a role in the future output of hydroelectric energy. FERC licensing requirements have been upgraded recently, and there is much debate on what impact this will have on existing facilities. The possibility of facilities requiring expensive work in order to meet current specifications, and the possibility of facilities simply not being relicensed, are both potential threats to this power supply.

It is clearly difficult to calculate the future contribution of hydroelectric

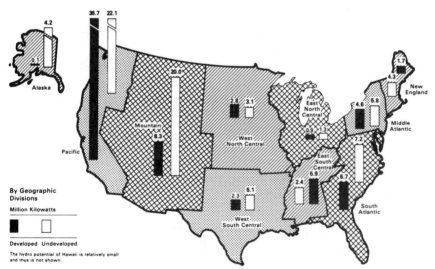

U.S. hydroelectric resources developed/undeveloped. (Reprinted with permission from the Federal Energy Regulatory Commission)

energy. Many factors have to be considered, and future regulatory and environmental decisions cannot be known. It is widely accepted, however, that its contibution is likely to decrease over time.

Costs

The costs involved in both current and future hydroelectric power generation are very site-specific. Construction costs, costs to adjust for environmental issues and the flow of the river and its resultant energy are all factors that play an important role in the ultimate cost of the energy generated from a specific location. Currently, hydropower is considered to be about the cheapest source of electricity available, but its cost is increasing.

As is common for renewable energy sources, up-front costs are relatively high, with lower operations and maintenance (O&M) costs. The capital costs for large projects have been estimated to be between $500 and $2,500 per kilowatt, with those for smaller facilities varying more widely, ranging from $1,000 to more than $6,000 per kilowatt. O&M costs range from $0.01 to $0.02 per kilowatt hour, depending on the size of the facility. The cost of electricity from newly constructed hydroelectric plants in 1989 was between $0.03 and $0.06 per kilowatt hour.

In the future, the costs will depend largely on what type of site is used. Retrofitting and upgrading existing sites is expected to be the cheapest strategy, followed by adding electrical facilities to existing dams with no hydroelectric facilities. Finally, the development of new sites is expected to be the most expensive. The costs involved with increased regulatory processes will affect all types of hydroelectric development.

Environmental Issues

The addition of a hydroelectric power station to a river, or even the retrofitting of hydroelectric facilities to an existing dam, can have harmful effects on the local ecosystem. (In general, large dams are more harmful to this ecosystem than are run-of-river facilities.) Fish and plant life are affected, as are water quality and the surrounding land.

Fish are affected because their spawning paths can be blocked by a dam and because the hydroelectric facility will affect the amount and timing of water flowing through a river, its temperature, and its oxygen content. The negative effect of industrialization on animal life has been evidenced in many locations. The Columbia River is a prime example: annual fish runs decreased from roughly ten to sixteen million in the preindustrial era of that river to 2.5 million by the late 1970s. Throughout the Northwest the effects of dams are causing great concern, particularly because the migration of several species of salmon that are protected as threatened or endangered is blocked by hydropower facilities.

The accumulation of sediments, mentioned previously, affects both the efficiency of the hydropower system at hand and the river's ecosystem. Since this sediment carries nutrients that benefit both fish and any agricultural areas that may be downstream, its blockage can deprive fish and other wildlife of needed food and agricultural land of vital nutrients. The water quality is affected in other ways, too. Changes in temperature, oxygen levels, or salt and mineral content also affect the river's ecosystem.

There are, of course, at least partial solutions to many of these problems. Fish ladders allow fish to bypass hydroelectric facilities and continue upstream; screens and other barriers can be mounted to keep fish and other animals from becoming entangled in the turbines; efforts can be made to keep the minimum flow rate of a river at a certain level. Temperature changes can be modified by careful placement of intake structures, and increased turbulence helps keep the oxygen level up. These techniques have the potential for mitigating many of the environmental concerns regarding hydroelectric power generation and are in fact being incorporated into new and retrofitted systems with increasing frequency.

In an attempt to avoid or minimize the environmental problems connected with hydropower, U.S. environmental legislation—notably the National Wild and Scenic Rivers Act of 1968—is making the development of hydropower sources more difficult—and more costly. Yet many would perhaps prefer the environmental impacts of a hydropower system over those of competing energy sources. For example, using hydropower does not create significant amounts of air pollution, whereas burning fossil fuels does. And unlike nuclear energy, hydropower produces no toxic waste.

Benefits

We have seen that despite the environmental concerns and the high up-front costs, hydropower eliminates worries about polluting emissions and dangerous waste. We have also seen that the O&M costs, and the hourly energy charge, are quite cheap in comparison to other sources. Another important advantage of hydropower is that it can be turned on quickly and the power output can be adjusted quickly. Finally, hydropower is supplied by a domestic resource base. It allows the owner country to be self-sufficient for a large part of its energy supply. Any country that develops its hydro resources is exploiting a domestic source, allowing it to rely less on outside sources. In the case of the United States, hydroelectric power has represented a very large resource base.

☐ OCEAN THERMAL ENERGY CONVERSION (OTEC)

Ocean thermal energy conversion, or OTEC, involves exploiting the temperature differences between warm surface water and colder, deeper layers. Particularly in tropical latitudes, the difference between the temperature on the surface and that of the water at depths of around 1,000 meters can vary by 68 degrees Fahrenheit or more. This temperature difference can be used to generate electricity by alternately vaporizing and condensing a working fluid.

A French physicist named Arsene d'Arsonval was the first to propose, in 1881, that electricity could be generated by exploiting the ocean's temperature differences. It was not until approximately fifty years later, however, that one of d'Arsonval's pupils, Georges Claude, actually attempted a practical application of the OTEC concept by building a small shore-based plant off the coast of Cuba.

The potential energy resource represented by OTEC technology is significant. The relative regularity of ocean temperatures means that OTEC systems can provide steady levels of power, which makes them suitable for baseload use (the minimum continuous power level used) by utilities. They also offer potential for remote shoreline locations that have little or no other energy options.

Because of the need for temperature variation, OTEC systems are only applicable to certain parts of the world. When annual temperature variations are taken into account, the usable OTEC thermal resource lies mainly between the tropics of Cancer and Capricorn, with the most attractive locations in the Pacific, where a large area has shown temperature differentials of seventy-five degrees Fahrenheit. The actual placement of a given facility can vary according to local specifications. For example, the system could be floating, land-based, or fixed on some sort of tower.

The Technology

There are two types of systems for converting the differences in ocean temperatures into energy: the closed-cycle system and the open-cycle system. The system first developed by d'Arsonval was based on a closed-cycle concept, but the one attempted by Claude fifty years later took that idea and developed it further, eventually coming up with an open-cycle system.

The two systems are relatively similar: OTEC works as a heat engine that uses warm seawater to vaporize a working fluid; the vapor then turns a turbine. Cold seawater pumped up from the ocean's lower levels condenses the vapor as it exits the turbine. The condensing process provides the impetus for the flow of the working fluid, which can be either the warm seawater or another fluid such as ammonia. In the latter case, the condensed vapor is pumped back to the evaporator, forming a closed cycle. In the former case, the condensed vapor is discharged.

Each system has its benefits and drawbacks. Opinion is divided as to which system is the best overall. Whereas some believe closed-cycle systems offer the best bet for short-term commercial application, others think that open-cycle plants will be the most cost-effective in the long run, especially considering the by-products, such as aquaculture and fresh water, associated with this technology. (These by-products are discussed in the Current Status section.)

Closed-cycle plants can use smaller turbines than the large, low-pressure turbines in an open-cycle system. Problems such as cost, corrosion, efficiency, and biofouling (when marine matter becomes trapped in the system) of heat exchangers have yet to be solved, however.

The open-cycle system is easier to build because it does not have to withstand such high pressure. Also in its favor is the potential for advantageous by-products such as aquaculture and desalinated water. The main disadvantages of this system, on the other hand, are that its components must be maintained under a high vacuum and that it requires a larger turbine (because the steam is much less dense than that of a typical closed-cycle working fluid). In addition, open-cycle plants with larger power-generating capabilities have yet to be developed. Because of its simplicity and lower costs, the U.S. Department of Energy has decided to focus its OTEC R&D on open-cycle systems. Most of this research is taking place in Hawaii (see the following section).

Hybrid systems also exist. These use the smaller condenser and turbine of a closed-cycle system and can produce desalinated water as in the open cycle.

There are many components to an OTEC system, many of which constitute well-developed technology, but some of which are still being researched. The major components being researched are the cold-water pipes and the heat exchangers. Areas of research for the cold-water pipes are corrosion and pressure-, temperature-, and stress-resistance. The inaccessibility of these pipes also causes maintenance problems. To overcome the actual structural problems associated with the pipes, experimentation with various materials is under way. Some of these materials include concrete, steel, aluminum, polyethylene, and other plastics.

The heat exchangers (the evaporator and the condensor) are considered the most expensive components for a closed-cycle OTEC system. The problems being investigated with these components include biofouling, corrosion, and durability. As with the cold-water pipes, various materials are being considered, including titanium and aluminum combinations, copper-nickel alloys, and various plastics.

Current Status

Demonstration OTEC systems have been set up in Japan, France, the United Kingdom, and Hawaii. The project in Hawaii, at the Natural

Energy Laboratory of Hawaii (NELH), is of particular interest because of the diversity of research being conducted there. In addition to working with both closed-cycle and open-cycle systems, Hawaii's center looks at spin-off industries that work alongside the OTEC technology and stand a good chance of making the system profitable.

Hawaii offers ideal conditions for OTEC: whereas surface waters tend to be around eighty degrees Fahrenheit, the temperature 2,000 feet below drops to forty-three degrees Fahrenheit. This has led to the development of research programs into both open- and closed-cycled systems at the NELH. The U.S. Department of Energy supports research into open-cycle systems, with the main focus of its research the development of two- to fifteen-megawatt open-cycle systems for use just offshore.

Some of the research at NELH focuses on alleviating problems that were discussed in the preceding section. Other efforts are directed at solving the problem of warm-water tubes in closed-cycle systems becoming clogged with marine organisms. One of the most interesting aspects of the research is the development of by-products such as desalination and aquaculture. These side industries promise to help make OTEC financially viable at a much faster rate than would otherwise be the case.

The potential for fresh water from OTEC is enormous. It has been estimated that a 100-megawatt plant in the right climate (such as in Hawaii) could produce about fifteen million gallons of fresh water daily. Aquaculture is another area with great potential. Alongside the OTEC researchers, entrepreneurs are producing a wide variety of products. These range from algae, which can be sold for biomedical applications, to salmon, lobster, abalone, oysters, sea urchins, and seaweeds. It is also worth noting that the buildings at NELH are air-conditioned by systems that use the cold seawater.

OTEC technology is being studied in other countries as well. As noted, Japan, France, and the United Kingdom—as well as Taiwan, India, and the Virgin Islands—all have research projects in various stages of development. The project in Hawaii is the most advanced, however. No commercial OTEC facilities are currently in existence, although it is estimated that this technology will enter the marketplace as a viable industry sometime in the 1990s.

Future Potential

OTEC certainly has a role to play in the future energy supply to many areas, particularly island nations and tropical coastal areas. Of particular interest to the United States: it has been stated that within the 1990–2000 time frame OTEC could supply substantial generating capacity for Hawaii, Puerto Rico, the Virgin Islands, Guam, Micronesia, and American Samoa. Island nations that must pay extremely high costs for fuel or that have limited energy sources are ideal markets for OTEC. In addition to smaller, remote applications, OTEC is also ideal for baseload energy generation, a benefit that separates it from many other renewable sources.

One of the advantages of OTEC (open-cycle) that makes its future success much more likely is its ability to engender by-products that can be extremely profitable in their own right. These activities greatly improve OTEC's overall cost-effectiveness while offering their own societal and economic benefits.

Costs

The high up-front costs of OTEC are hampering its development. The initial equipment, especially the evaporator, condenser, and cold-water pipe, comprises approximately 70 percent of the OTEC system cost. Maintenance costs may also be higher than those for conventional fuel-fired plants, but in the long run this energy source can be very cost-effective, for several reasons. First, OTEC fuel costs are nonexistent, so depending on the life of an OTEC plant, long-term costs come down dramatically. This technology is also particularly appropriate for smaller nations, which usually pay significantly higher costs for fuel to generate electricity, as noted above. In these instances OTEC is expected to be able to provide a cost-effective source for generating energy.

The ability to attract funding is an ongoing problem for OTEC facilities. The combination of a slow return on investment and the fact that OTEC facilities are still in the demonstration phase, with no commercial plants in existence, makes it difficult to obtain financing. Government or cooperative international financing may well be needed to overcome this obstacle. It has been estimated that if investors could be sure that an OTEC plant would run for thirty years without major overhauls, they would jump at the chance to build such plants today. But the lack of an observable history of OTEC technology for that period of time makes investors hesitate.

Environmental Issues

There are several environmental aspects of OTEC that must be taken into consideration. These revolve around the release of either chemicals or waste water back into the surrounding ocean.

In closed-cycle systems there is a danger of the working fluid escaping into the surrounding sea if the system is floating, or into the ground, if it is land-based. Clearly, precautions can be taken to reduce this risk. In addition, since heat exchangers are cleaned by intermittent chlorination, concerns have been expressed about chlorine being released into the surrounding environment. It is possible, however, to collect the chlorine without releasing it.

The discharge of warm or cold water into surrounding water with a different temperature is also a concern. Current technology allows developers to release water back into appropriate temperatures, so this need not be a problem if handled properly. Still, some experts have expressed concern that interfering with deep ocean water could have unforeseen environmental effects.

Finally, the effect of an OTEC system on the surrounding fish is a subject of some speculation. Some fish eggs and larvae may become trapped in the system, which might affect the local distribution of these species. Likewise, changes in local salinity and temperature might affect the local ecosystem. According to the International Energy Agency, however, studies show that these effects are limited.

Benefits

The environmental concerns discussed above are considered to be relatively minor and appear to be controllable. More important is the fact that OTEC is a renewable source that causes no pollution or greenhouse gases. Additional benefits are both economic and political. OTEC offers the potential of economically valuable by-products as well as a degree of self-sufficiency to the nations who develop its enormous energy. Finally, the constant supply of OTEC energy gives it an advantage over those renewable energy sources that are slightly less regular in their production of energy.

As with other renewable energy sources, OTEC will have to overcome hurdles of financing in order to obtain widespread application. The technology is largely in place for this energy source to be developed, however, and it is expected to play a role in our future energy supply.

□ WAVE ENERGY

Waves are created by the wind affecting the ocean's surface. The amount of energy that can be extracted from a wave depends on the height of the wave (the amount of water the wind displaces from the ocean's mean surface level) and the speed of the created waves. The energy from a wave is proportional to the square of the wave height. So, a two-foot wave has four times the energy, and a three-foot wave has nine times the energy, of a one-foot wave, for example. Wave energy devices take this energy from the waves and convert it to either electrical or mechanical energy.

As with OTEC, the potential for wave energy is stronger in certain parts of the globe. The area between the latitudes of forty degrees and sixty degrees in both the northern and southern hemispheres offers the greatest potential for wave energy. Another important factor is what is known as the "fetch"—the distance over which the wind has blown over the sea, without interruption, before reaching the point of interest.

Shorelines located at the end of a long fetch have the potential for significant wave energy. The shorelines of certain countries are both in the proper location within the noted latitudes as well as at the end of a fetch, making them ideal for the development of wave energy. Some of the most favorable locations are the eastern coastline of Japan and the western coastlines of Scotland, Norway, and the United States.

The first historical reference to our interest in using the energy inherent in waves is thought to date back to July 12, 1799. The first patent for a wave energy device was filed on this date in Paris by a father and son named Girard. The device registered by the Girards was not too dissimilar to devices being studied in the early 1980s. From the late eighteenth century to the last couple of decades, however, not much work was done on this technology. One of the earliest schemes in recent years was studied on the island of Mauritius. Research began on a project that theoretically could have provided all the power needed for the island's entire population, but the project was canceled in 1966 because of declining oil prices.

The Technology

Wave energy can be produced either from a device floating on the ocean's surface or from a power plant fixed to the ground. A fixed plant can be either land-based or located offshore. Of the numerous wave energy devices invented and tested in recent years, most fall into three main categories: surface followers, pressure-activated devices, and focusing devices.

Surface followers use a mechanical connection between a device that floats on the ocean's surface and a fixed pivot to convert the rising and falling motions of the wave into electricity. An example of a surface follower is a device known as Salter's Duck, developed by Stephen Salter of the University of Edinburgh in Scotland. The European Community is studying the viability of his duck, which bobs up and down on the ocean's surface to extract the waves' energy. Salter's Duck has demonstrated an absorption efficiency of more than 80 percent.

Pressure-activated devices use the changing water level to produce varying pressure. An example of this type of mechanism is one that uses the pressure changes to push air through an air turbine, which then turns to produce electricity. An oscillating water column (OWC) is a pressure-activated wave energy device. It works from both the rise and fall of the waves. When the water level in the column rises, air is pushed through a turbine. Then, when the water level drops, air is sucked into the turbine from the atmosphere. The turbine spins in the same direction no matter which way the air comes from, so it can work as water rises or falls in the water column. OWCs have been built for less than $1,900 per kilowatt, and the device has generated power for $0.04 to $0.06 per kilowatt hour—rates competitive with other current energy sources.

Focusing devices use physical barriers to redirect waves, focusing their energy toward a particular point and strengthening their power. To be more specific: the waves are directed into a narrow, steep channel, which pushes the water up high enough so that it can spill down into a catch basin; the water can then be released through a turbine to create electricity. Although focusing devices are the simplest of the wave energy technologies, they are thought to have excellent potential for producing large quantities of energy.

Current Status

It is only in the last decade or two that wave energy has been looked at seriously as a potential source of electrical or hydraulic energy. Despite this short history, technological developments in the field have been impressive.

Norway brought the first two wave power plants on-line in 1986. One of these plants is a focusing device, a 5,500-square-meter reservoir that is open to the sea in a tapered channel, while the other is a pressure-activated device, an oscillating water column. The two wave plants have a combined capacity of about one megawatt. Although these are proto-type designs, the manufacturers of the oscillating water column do offer their system for sale commercially. The success of these plants has prompted orders for similar ones from several other countries: Portugal and Indonesia, for example, have concluded contracts to purchase wave energy devices.

Japan also has been using wave energy devices for several years, though on a smaller scale. Hundreds of small navigational buoys with generating capacities of approximately 0.5 to three kilowatts are used in the seas around this country. Several other countries use small numbers of these buoys also. Although there are relatively few working models of wave energy around the globe, several countries are working on the technology. These include Japan, Scotland, Norway, Great Britain, and India.

Japan has been the location of several international research projects into wave energy. A forty-kilowatt seabed fixed wave-power generator was installed in 1983 near a town called Sanze. Past studies have also tested a floating wave-power generator in the form of a barge called *Kaimei*. Both projects allowed researchers to gain useful information about the workings of these types of wave generation plants.

Kaimei was built in 1976 by the Japan Marine Science Technology Center and adopted as an international project by the International Energy Agency. Its first stage of testing began in the late 1970s; then, following several years of inactivity, *Kaimei* began its work again in 1985. The length of time from *Kaimei*'s construction to the end of its second testing period was about ten years—time to gain significant information about the character of waves and of the device itself. Initial *Kaimei* testing demonstrated the feasibility of large-scale wave power generation and yielded a successful small-scale transmission of generated power to land-based facilities. It aslo showed that a floating-type wave power system can have a long life: the hull, the moorings, the power cable to shore, the turbines, and the generators all came through the testing period in good condition, with only minor problems. Wave power tests aboard *Kaimei* have led researchers involved in that project to say that wave energy could theoretically generate the equivalent of up to 50 percent of Japan's energy needs.

The Sanze shore-fixed wave power generator was installed after the *Kaimei* testing was finished. This generator was an oscillating water column (OWC) device. Performance of this system was judged superior to that of the Kaimei barge. Over a period of one week the system generated average electrical power ranging from thirty to forty kilowatts for two days, from ten to fifteen kilowatts for two days, from three to five kilowatts for two days, and one kilowatt or less for one day.

The European Community, after refusing to fund wave energy research for years, suddenly changed its mind in 1991 and began to fund feasibility studies within that organization's member countries. Researchers have long thought that Europe offers great potential for wave energy production. Surveys have shown that there is a potential 110 gigawatts (equivalent to roughly 85 percent of the present EC electricity demand) of wave power available along Europe's coastlines. Specific countries (Ireland, Scotland, and Portugal) could theoretically receive all their electricity from wave power.

So far, small generators for buoys and lighthouses are commercially available, as is the Norwegian oscillating device. Other devices are all still in some stage of research and demonstration.

Future Potential

The potential of wave energy is great, particularly in those countries within the correct latitudes and at the end of long fetches. Studies have shown that wave energy will eventually be able to contribute greatly to the energy supply of many of these countries.

Small-scale wave energy generators, with capacities of 100 watts to one kilowatt, are expected to be produced in increasing numbers over the next few years. Also, shore-based wave power converters are expected to be put to practical use in the near future. The oscillating water column device appears to be the most technically advanced from both cost and performance standpoints.

One of the issues to be tackled with wave energy systems is the need for the facilities to withstand tremendous storms, even if these occurrences are rare. For example, although the average wave may be about two feet along the mid-Atlantic coast of the United States, a plant built here would need to be able to withstand a twenty-foot storm wave, even if that storm wave were expected only rarely.

Because of the irregularity of waves, this energy source is not expected to be applied to utility baseload generation. It certainly has applications for remote power supplies and in specific coastal areas, however. The issue of irregularity can be addressed, as with other renewable energy sources, with the inclusion of energy storage. Also, spreading wave energy devices out over larger stretches of ocean is likely to catch more diverse energy, so one site can produce while another is inactive due to calm seas.

Although electricity generation has been the main focus of wave energy research to date, other uses have been suggested, with some research undertaken in these directions. Such possible alternative uses include employing wave energy to create hydrogen and ammonia from seawater, refining aluminum, and converting wave energy into hydraulic power for transmission ashore.

Costs

Estimates on the cost of energy from wave energy projects vary widely. The developer of the Seamill, a relatively new windmill-type device that spins underwater, estimates that his device will produce electricity for as little as $0.015 to $0.03 per hour. The theory behind such a device is that it would work in a similar manner to real windmills, but the power in currents is typically ten times more concentrated than that in wind. Others calculate the cost of wave energy to be as much as three times that estimate.

Because there are still relatively few commercial applications, more time will be needed to get an accurate assessment of the costs involved. Another factor that makes estimates difficult is that the specific wave conditions at each potential location will be different and will therefore affect costs. The oscillating water column used in Norway has been shown to generate electricity there for $0.04 to $0.06 per kilowatt hour. If this is any indication, the outlook for the cost-competitiveness of at least this specific technology is good.

As with many of the water-based renewable energy sources discussed in this chapter, costs for wave energy technologies are heaviest at the outset, with the construction and installation of the devices. Maintenance costs must also be considered, but the energy source over the life of the system is free.

Environmental Issues

It is difficult to make generalizations about environmental impact of wave energy technology for two reasons: as of this date, relatively little research has been done on this issue; moreover, there are a variety of different types of devices being developed in the field. Nevertheless, it is possible to offer a few observations about mechanical floating devices and barrier devices.

Mechanical floating devices are considered overall to have very little environmental impact. The only potential danger would be if a device broke loose from its anchor and presented a navigational hazard. Even if the device did not break loose, if it is small and close to the water surface level, it may be difficult to detect and hence create a hazard. This problem can be easily solved, however, by the addition of some kind of light or electronic signal attached to the device on top of a pole.

Barrier devices are more likely to cause some kind of environmental changes, whether on- or offshore. They will probably change local wave and tidal patterns slightly, which may have an effect on some species in the local beach ecosystem. Likewise, the migration habits of some species of fish may be affected.

Benefits

Unlike energy generated by fossil fuels, wave energy does not produce harmful emissions or by-products. And because the ocean's waves are a constant, renewable source of energy, harnessing power from them eliminates the danger of using up the earth's precious resources. Wave energy is potentially more valuable than wind energy as an energy source: waves don't come and go in a gust; they develop gradually, over great distances and long periods of time, and they remain long after the wind which helped create them is gone.

The fact that wave energy does not use up valuable, finite natural resources, that is it nonpolluting, and that its production is not danger-ous does not make it unique. Clearly, the same can be said for many other renewable energy sources. Waves also offer the potential for supply-ing power to isolated locations that have no other energy source or only a limited energy source.

While the various technologies currently available to harness the energy inherent in waves still need developmental work, they show promise and can be counted on to play a part in future energy supplies.

☐ TIDAL ENERGY

Tides are created by the gravity of the sun, the moon, and the earth's rotation. These bodies moving in relation to one another create annual tidal cycles around the globe. Tides are affected by a variety of elements. The annual tidal cycles affect the range of tides at certain times of the year, and local geographical features such as shelving, funneling, reflec-tion, and resonance play an important role as well.

The actual energy available from tides is generated from the kinetic energy of the water moving from a higher to a lower elevation in a fashion not too dissimilar to that of hydroelectric dams. In tidal energy systems, the water is captured as it rises and is later released and directed through turbines, which then generate electricity. The power that can be harnessed from tides is proportional to the square of the tide's range. So, for example, a three-meter tide generates nine times as much power as a one-meter tide.

Tidal power has, in fact, been used in the past to provide mechanical energy. It is only in recent years that it has been looked at as a possible source for the generation of electricity. As early as the twelfth century, people used tidal power to create mechanical energy, with mills. The first tidal mills were found along the north Atlantic coasts of Europe, in Brittany, Andalusia, and England. Colonial New England also used small tidal energy plants (up to 100 kilowatts of mechanical power) as early as 1609 to power lumber- and gristmills.

The Technology

There are two main designs for tidal power generation. These are ebb generation and two-way generation. A third design—flood generation—exists as well, but it is not considered to be practical.

Ebb generation allows the water to flow through channels into a barrage (artificial dam) as the tide rises. All passageways are closed soon after high tide to trap the water, which is held behind the barrage until the tide has dropped enough to allow for a sufficient difference in water level between the trapped water and the ocean. At this point the water is released, and as it flows through the turbines it generates electricity. When the water levels on either side of the barrage get too close, the system is closed down until the time is right to start catching the water again, at which point the process begins again. This is the most common method of generating tidal energy.

Two-way generation produces energy in the same way as ebb generation, but it can also generate energy as the tide flows the other way. This presents the advantage of offering a longer period during which generation can occur, but its disadvantages—namely, higher initial expense, the production of slightly less energy than ebb generation, and disturbances to ports and navigation—make it relatively uncommon.

Tidal power technology is proven; the mechanisms used are part of well-established technology, and the test sites around the world have demonstrated the effectiveness of the concept. According to the International Energy Agency, there is little need for further research and development in this field. It only remains to apply the technology to suitable sites around the world.

Current Status

Although this energy source is still relatively uncommon, it may surprise many to learn that there are actually several tidal power plants in operation around the globe. The world's largest tidal plant (with a capacity of 240 megawatts) is in La Rance estuary in northern France. The La Rance tidal power station has operated since its completion in 1968 with an overall availability rate of 93 percent. Another major tidal energy test facility, the twenty-megawatt Annapolis Tidal Power Project at Annapolis Royal in Nova Scotia (on the Bay of Fundy), operated in its first year (1984) with 99 percent availability. Both these sites have provided invaluable information to researchers and have proven the viability of this energy source.

The La Rance plant is the only plant operating today on a commercial basis, but several countries are developing tidal power through a series of feasibility studies that show promise. The former Soviet Union built a small 400-kilowatt demonstration plant at Kislaya Guba in 1967. The former Soviet Union, Canada, France, the United States (Hawaii), and China are home to most of the tidal energy development today.

Studies to date have shown that tidal plants must be located in areas with a mean tidal range of more than sixteen feet before power can be produced (with current technology). The sites must also provide a large amplitude (the difference between the high- and low-water marks) of the tides and the possibility of creating large reservoirs to store a great quantity of power-producing water.

Future Potential

The potential for tidal power is significant. The International Energy Agency has estimated that the various tidal projects worldwide could theoretically produce 635,000 gigawatt hours of energy. Certain areas around the globe have been identified as offering the greatest potential for tidal energy production. Some of these are the Bay of Fundy in Canada and the United States; Cook Inlet in Alaska; Chausey in the Bay of Mont St. Michael in France; the Gulf of Mazen in the former Soviet Union; the Severn River Estuary in England; the Walcott Inlet in Australia; San Jose, Argentina; and Asan Bay in South Korea. In the Bay of Fundy, for example, it is usual for tides to vary as much as thirty-five to forty feet, and extreme tides can be more than fifty feet. It has been said that the total flow at each tide through the Bay of Fundy could theoretically generate 400 million kilowatt hours of energy, approximately the same output as 250 large nuclear plants.

Several of the aforementioned sites have already been developed for feasibility studies. The Severn River Estuary has, in fact, been the site of major tidal energy feasibility studies over the past several years. If current plans go ahead, this Severn Barrage Project would be the world's largest tidal power system, approximately ten miles long and capable of producing 7,200 megawatts of power.

While most researchers have looked at estuaries as target locations for tidal barrages, some believe "open coast" schemes might be preferable. These would be located in large areas of shallow coastal water, perhaps as far as five or six miles from the shore. Proponents of open coast facilities believe these would have less environmental impact, cost less, and might even be used as bases for offshore wind plants.

The future of tidal power generation is largely dependent on the availability of development funds. While the technology has been proven, it takes significant funds, usually of the size only available from government sources, to finance the initial construction costs of these power stations. Feasibility studies underway in Russia, China, and elsewhere may well encourage investors, as more and more stations prove themselves to work efficiently and reliably.

Costs

As noted, the costs involved in developing tidal energy projects are very high initially. The difficulty in raising the investment needed for its development has been one of the reasons for the relatively slow development of this energy source.

When looked at over the life of a project, however, the costs associated with tidal energy can be very appealing. It is important to remember that with this kind of energy source there are no fuel costs. The Severn Tidal Power Group consortium, which studied the initial feasibility of the Severn Barrage, estimated its initial construction costs at $8.25 billion, but expected the plant to be able to produce power at a cost of $0.045 per kilowatt hour (compared with $0.06 per kilowatt hour for coal).

Environmental Issues

Feasibility studies for the Severn Barrage Project have been paying particular attention to the potential environmental side effects of a tidal power station there. These side effects—both pro and con—can be said to hold true for tidal power stations in general.

Tidal energy systems offer the same sorts of environmental benefits that have been discussed for solar and wind energy systems: they avoid the pollution that comes from burning fossil fuels; they are renewable (because the ocean is a constant source of energy); and hence they do not use up any of our precious natural resources.

Among the concerns about tidal power plants are endangerment to bird and fish species, changes in wetland ecosystems, and the accumulation of pollutants. All these concerns are clearly site-specific and need to be studied in detail on a case-by-case basis. (It must be noted, however, that the placement of a barrier can affect a great area of ocean and shore. Computer models demonstrating the possible effects of a barrier in the Bay of Fundy, for example, have predicted that the whole of the Gulf of Maine would be affected by the placement of such a barrier.)

With regard to birds, the construction of a barrage, which will change the water levels on either side, will naturally change the local ecosystem. Strong tidal currents tend to uplift and redeposit bottom sediments, a phenomenon that can be halted by the intrusion of a large barrier. If certain plant and animal species cannot survive in the new environment, the birds and fish that feed on them will also perish. With fish, a specific concern is that they will be unable to migrate up rivers fitted with a barrier.

The accumulation of pollutants is another concern. Rivers with a barrage will be "flushed" less often, leading to a buildup of pollutants. The resultant drop in oxygen supply could mean danger to the rivers' inhabitants.

Disruption to navigation and boating systems has also been mentioned as a concern. Such issues must also be addressed when studying the possible development of tidal energy power stations.

Decison makers will need to weigh the benefits offered by tidal energy with any potential changes to ecosystems caused by the imposition of large barrages on a site-by-site basis. The technology and research is largely in place, and several large projects are being studied. If the problem of high initial costs can be overcome, it appears that tidal energy may well be a part of our future energy base.

The various types of water-based renewable energy sources discussed in this chapter offer a wide range of options for future energy planners. While these are certainly not exempt from environmental concerns, it is generally accepted that they offer less upset than their conventional counterparts. Financing is still an issue in many cases, as is continued research and development. These technologies are in varying stages of readiness, but on the whole they all look promising as potential future energy sources.

Benefits

As opposed to some alternative energy sources, the tides are a constant, and tidal power can be provided continuously. (This does not mean that it can be lined up with the daily peak needs of utilities, however, because tides change slightly each day as part of their cycle.) So once the initial costs have been put out, the energy is free and continuous. The tidal stations are expected to have long lifetimes—of up to 120 years. The amount of energy produced is also enormous. In England, the Energy

Technology Support Unit estimated in 1988 that the potential of tidal power in that country alone could be as much as fifty terrawatt hours per year (just under 20 percent of electricity demand at that time).

The use of tidal power from the waters around a country allows that country a degree of energy self-sufficiency, always an advantage in a world where fossil fuel prices and availability can be unstable. The environmental benefits of using tidal power over more conventional methods can also be significant.

4 GEOTHERMAL ENERGY

Geothermal energy is heat generated by natural processes within the earth. It can be contained in underground reservoirs of steam, hot water, hot saline fluids, and hot dry rock. It is estimated that 10 percent of the world's land mass contains accessible hydrogeothermal resources that could theoretically provide several million quads of energy every year. Strictly speaking, geothermal energy is not renewable on a human time scale. But because the resource is so large, it is treated as inexhaustible.

There are three main original sources of geothermal energy. The largest amount of heat is released from the decay of naturally radioactive elements that have built up throughout the earth's history; it is estimated that 45 to 85 percent of the heat escaping from the earth is due to such radioactive decay in the crust. The remaining significant sources of internal heat are the heat of impact and compression from the earth's initial formation and heat released from the sinking of heavy metals such as iron, nickel, and copper as they descended to form the earth's core.

While the occurrence of geothermal heat is normal at great depths within the earth, its existence close to or at the surface is less common. It is in these locations, however, that we are able to witness the tremendous energy that is trapped within our planet. Volcanoes and geysers are examples of geothermal energy that has traveled up from deep within the earth and surfaced. It is also in these locations that we are currently able to harness geothermal energy. These geothermal resources typically have three components: an unusual concentration of some heat source; a fluid that transports the heat from the rock within the earth to the surface; and permeability in the rock sufficient to allow the development of a flow system through which the fluid can circulate.

The unusual concentration of heat typically comes from the intrusion of molten rock (magma) from deep within the earth's surface to levels closer to the surface, or from the ascent of groundwater. Most of the time, the liquid that transports the heat either has originated from the water that was trapped during the initial formation of the rock or has percolated from the surface down through faults and various gaps under the earth's surface. The permeability, or rock's capacity to spread fluid, is made possible through pores or open spaces created by fractures and faults within the earth.

One area of particularly active geothermal and volcanic activity is called the Ring of Fire, a large semicircular belt surrounding the Pacific Ocean. The Ring of Fire follows the Pacific Plate, one of the many plates making up the earth's surface. It borders the Philippines, Japan, the Aleutian Islands, and the western edges of North, Central, and South America and is responsible for much of the geothermal activity in these areas. Earthquakes, volcanoes, and geysers are common along the Ring of Fire.

☐ HISTORY OF GEOTHERMAL ENERGY

In early times geothermal sites were mainly used for heated mineral baths, spas, and other medicinal purposes. We have since developed several other uses for geothermal energy. For example, in the 1890s the city of Boise, Idaho began using geothermal energy to heat homes. The Italians were the first to use geothermal steam to generate electricity, with a five-kilowatt system in 1904 in a town called Larderello, where geothermal electricity is still being produced. The Larderello site had also been used for industrial heating and mechanical power before it began to generate electricity.

The United States followed Italy in developing geothermal electricity by developing The Geysers geothermal field in California in 1916. New Zealand was the next country to develop its geothermal energy potential, and these three countries dominated the development of geothermal energy until the early 1960s.

The annual rate of growth of geothermal electrical power production was approximately 8 percent before 1978, when it increased to its peak of approximately 16 percent. Today that rate has slowed to between 8 and 10 percent annually.

☐ THE TECHNOLOGY

Geothermal energy can theoretically be captured in four different forms. Although only one of these forms is commercially available today, the others are undergoing research and development as potential energy sources.

Hydrothermal

The geothermal energy used today is hydrothermal energy. It consists of reservoirs of hot water and steam that are trapped in fractured rock or sediment beneath the earth's crust. This energy can be utilized in two ways: at high temperatures, it is used to generate electricity; and at low to moderate temperatures, it is used to provide direct heat. While the second application is the most widespread, both can be employed throughout the world.

Hydrothermal wells can be of two types: dry steam and hot water. Although wells with dry steam are of higher quality than those with hot water, the number of potential sites is very limited. The two main sources of dry steam located to date are at Larderello in Italy and The Geysers in California. Hot-water wells are more widely available, and they are gradually being used more and more frequently.

Hydrothermal reservoirs are found anywhere between several hundred and 14,000 feet below the earth's surface. The temperature of the fluids trapped inside ranges from approximately ninety to 680 degrees Fahrenheit. These reservoirs are the only ones currently tapped for geothermal energy because they are the easiest to access and therefore exploit. Within the United States, hydrothermal resource development has taken place predominantly in the western states, although some potential exists in other parts of the country as well.

High resource temperatures of above 300 degrees Fahrenheit are usually used to generate electricity. Depending on the state of the geothermal resource (vapor or liquid) and its temperature, one of three different technologies can be used to create electricity. If the source contains dry steam, the steam is cleaned as it comes out of the ground and then fed directly into a turbine-generator. If the source contains hydrothermal liquids hotter than 400 degrees Fahrenheit, flash steam technology is typically used: the water is allowed to flash into steam as it exits the earth's surface, and the steam then drives a turbine. Finally, for sources with liquids at moderate temperatures and those with a high degree of salinity, a relatively new binary cycle technology is employed. In this process the hot liquid is kept under pressure by a pump and then vaporizes a secondary working fluid such as a hydrocarbon, which in turn works a turbine. The fluid is then repressurized in a closed-loop system.

Geothermal electric plants can also have hybrid designs. These combine geothermal energy with supplemental energy from another source, such as biomass or fossil fuels. Hybrid systems are usually appropriate only for cooler temperature reservoirs that may need additional energy; sources with high temperatures do not need supplemental energy.

Lower temperature resources have a variety of direct heat applications. Most commonly, direct geothermal heat is used for space heating in individual buildings or district heating, as is done in Iceland. (Reykjavik has been heated for forty years by geothermal energy.) Further uses include heat pumps, which can be used for space heating and cooling and are more efficient than air-source heat pumps; food processing; industrial applications; greenhouses; and fish hatcheries.

Geopressured

Geopressured systems are another form of geothermal energy. These reservoirs contain hot fluids that are saturated in methane and locked with high pressure in layers of sandstone at depths of 10,000 to 20,000 feet below the earth's surface. The best-known source of geopressured energy in the United States is located along the Gulf Coast of Texas and Louisiana.

Although approximately 20 percent of the U.S. geothermal energy resource is in the form of geopressured reservoirs, researchers have thus far been unable to harness this energy economically. The great depth of these sources and the pressure involved cause problems that have kept costs high. Nevertheless, research projects have demonstrated the feasibility of geopressured energy sources. These resources are capable of supplying both heat and mechanical energy, in addition to methane gas. Wells in the Gulf Coast region have produced 700 million standard cubic feet of natural gas since 1985, and a one-megawatt power plant capable of converting methane and thermal energy into electricity was opened in 1989.

Hot Dry Rock

Hot dry rock is another potential source of geothermal energy that has yet to be commercially exploited. This resource is found where the earth's crust is thin and the magma is close enough to the surface to heat rock that contains very little water. Areas with hot dry rock are the most widely distributed and abundant source of geothermal energy, constituting approximately 70 percent of the U.S. geothermal resource. Once again, however, economical methods of capturing this energy source have yet to be developed. Current research involves drilling two wells; the first is injected with cool water, which circulates through rock fractures (all the time capturing heat from the rock) and comes back out through the second. The cool water is then reinjected.

Most is known about the hot dry rock resources in the western part of the United States, and this area is expected to be developed first. Demonstration projects have shown the feasibility of geothermal energy production from hot dry rock resources; tests are currently under way in New Mexico and in Great Britain.

Magma

Magma is the very hot molten rock below the earth's crust. It can reach temperatures of approximately 2,000 degrees Fahrenheit. Magma can theoretically be used for geothermal energy in the places where it is located at accessible depths (10,000 to 30,000 feet) below the earth's crust. Recent tests on a shallow lava field in Hawaii have demonstrated the feasibility of extracting energy from magma, but techniques to extract the energy from this source and to locate and use it commercially are still very much in the experimental stage. A magma well is also being tested in California. Energy from magma is expected to be the most difficult of all the geothermal energy types to develop. Magma energy development for the electricity sector and cogeneration (the sequential production of electricity and heat or steam from the same fuel source) currently occurs only in the western part of the United States.

Current Technology

While early exploration relied mainly on visual signs of geothermal energy—escaping steam or hot springs—researchers now use sophisticated methods and equipment to find suitable sources. Modern techniques to locate and confirm geothermal sources involve surveying geologic maps, using gravity meters to determine rock density, electrical methods to measure sound waves traveling through the earth, geochemical thermometers, and heat flow experiments.

When a possible source is located, drilling and production testing help to confirm the source and determine its potential. Whether the reservoir holds dry steam or liquid, its temperature range, and its degree of salinity are all important, but difficult, factors to determine. Yet these must be determined before any attempts to harness the energy can begin.

Much of the technology used to extract geothermal heat has been taken from the oil and gas industries, but there is still a need for some technological innovation specifically for geothermal development. The future development of hot dry rock, geopressured brine, and magma will certainly benefit from exploration and extraction developments in related fields.

To help work toward the extraction of currently unobtainable energy sources, research and development projects focus on newer technologies to facilitate the development of these sources. Better equipment is needed to forecast the performance of geopressured reservoirs and to explore magma deposits, and special drilling equipment must be developed for use in particularly hard rock, extreme salinity, and high temperatures. Current techniques for assessing the potential of reservoirs should also be perfected.

□ APPLICATIONS

As noted, geothermal resources with high temperatures are used for the generation of electricity. A power station is erected at the site, and then typically the power is transferred over a grid system. In the United States, most of these sources are located in the West.

Direct heat applications can use significantly lower temperatures than other geothermal energy applications. Resources with lower temperatures are far more widespread and hence can be tapped in many locations throughout the United States and the world. The accompanying table shows countries that have developed at least some of their geothermal resource for such applications.

The use of direct geothermal heat is increasing throughout the United States in particular: in the last ten years forty-five states have experienced significant development of direct use applications. The annual energy use of geothermal direct heat in the United States equals approximately five million barrels of oil. Direct heat projects can be found across the country. For example, in Elko, Nevada, a district heating system has been in place and working effectively since 1982. The system supplies heat to fourteen buildings and a sewage treatment plant. Another project (a large system for space and domestic water heating) supplies 550 individual homes in Klamath Falls, Oregon. The accompanying map shows the location of direct heat projects throughout the United States.

DIRECT GEOTHERMAL ENERGY UTILIZATION

Direct uses for fourteen countries having a capacity above 100 MWt thermal in 1990. All other countries are lumped under "Other."

COUNTRY	POWER (MWT)	ENERGY (GWH)	LOAD (%)
Bulgaria	293	770	30
China	2,143	5,527	29
Czechoslovakia	105	276	30
France	337	886	30
Hungary	1,276	3,554	30
Iceland	774	4,290	63
Italy	329	1,937	36
Japan	3,321	8,730	33
New Zealand	258	1,484	78
Romania	251	987	45
Former USSR	1,133	2,978	30
Turkey	246	625	29
United States[a]	2,195	5,505	29
Yugoslavia	113	602	61
Other	343	1,761	58
Total	13,117	39,912	35[b]

a. U.S. totals include ground-source heat pumps and thermal enhanced oil recovery.

b. Based on total thermal power and energy.

(Reprinted with permission from GRC Bulletin *and the Geo-Heat Center, Oregon Institute of Technology.)*

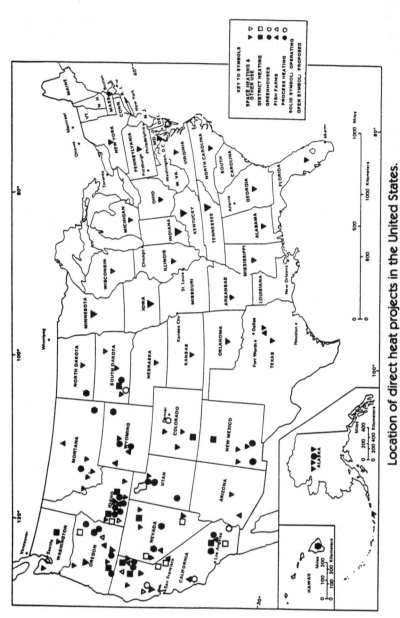

Location of direct heat projects in the United States.

(REPRINTED WITH PERMISSION FROM PAUL J. LIENAU/GEO-HEAT CENTER,
OREGON INSTITUTE OF TECHNOLOGY)

Included under "space heating and other uses" are ground-source heat pumps, which are being used in nearly all states now.

The geothermal heat pump (GHP) is the most efficient active technology for heating and air-conditioning homes: for each residential GHP installed, a utility can lower its overall energy generation by five kilowatts. These pumps use the earth's natural heat to adjust house temperatures and heat water through the use of a long plastic loop installed to a depth of up to several hundred feet into the ground. The loop is filled with water or some antifreeze solution that circulates between the heat pump and the ground, either removing heat from or returning heat to the ground, as required.

Since 1980, geothermal heat pumps have been the fastest-growing segment of the geothermal direct heat market, increasing its share from less than 10 percent to over 30 percent by 1990. Several major utilities and states provide financial incentives to encourage customers to install GHPs. The energy efficiency of these pumps benefits utilities and consumers alike.

Greenhouses can benefit from direct geothermal heat. Vegetables, flowers, houseplants, and tree seedlings are all grown successfully with direct heat systems. The use of direct heat allows greenhouses to be productive year-round in colder climates at cost-effective rates. One project near Helena, Montana, that raises roses has cut heating costs by 80 percent and overall costs by 35 percent by the introduction of geothermal heat.

Aquaculture is another successful application of direct geothermal energy. By 1991, there were aquaculture projects using geothermal water in seven western states. Typical species grown in these environments include catfish, bass, trout, freshwater prawns, and tropical fish. Because it can use relatively low geothermal temperatures—often as low as seventy degrees Fahrenheit—the potential for the widespread development of aquaculture is very good. Already there are signs of the increasing use of this particular geothermal application: in 1990 catfish processing increased by 21 percent.

Geothermal heat can also be used in a variety of industrial applications. These uses typically require temperatures significantly higher than those for direct heat applications. Examples of industrial uses include enhanced oil recovery (200 degrees Fahrenheit), operations to extract precious metals (230 degrees Fahrenheit), pulp and paper processing (400 degrees Fahrenheit), and timber drying (200 degrees Fahrenheit).

□ CURRENT STATUS

The United States is the world's largest producer of electricity from geothermal energy. The production of geothermal energy in this country

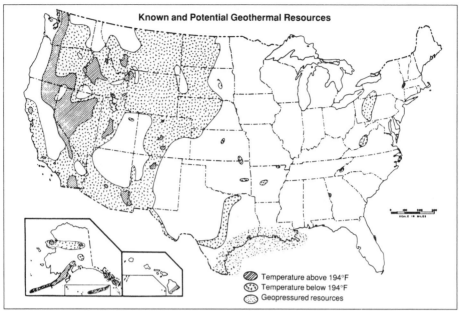

Known and Potential Geothermal Resources

Temperature above 194°F
Temperature below 194°F
Geopressured resources

Geothermal resources in the United States.

Known and potential U.S. geothermal resources. (Reprinted with permission from the National Renewable Energy Laboratory)

represents the energy equivalent of sixty million barrels of oil each year. Geothermal generation supplies about 7 percent of all of California's electricity and provides power in two other states.

In addition to the United States, about twenty foreign countries have developed geothermal energy to some degree (see accompanying table). The Philippines, Mexico, and Italy are the other major producers of geothermal energy. Most geothermal plants range from small (one to five megawatts) to medium-sized (twenty-five to sixty megawatts) facilities, while there are some as large as 110 megawatts.

The Geysers

Until recently, activity in the United States focused largely on The Geysers (in Sonoma County, California), which has been a successful commercial venture for two decades. Wells up to two miles deep capture the steam from this vast energy source. The site was discovered in 1847 by an explorer-surveyor and became a minor tourist attraction for some years until its eventual development as an energy source earlier this century.

The Geysers geothermal field covers an area of approximately thirty square miles. Its capacity of 2,050 megawatts makes it the largest geothermal development in the world today. Several companies operate out of The Geysers geothermal field. PG&E, with nineteen individual plants at this one site, obtains approximately 8.8 percent of its power

GEOTHERMAL ELECTRIC POWER

Capacity (MW)

COUNTRY	1980	1990	1995
China	0	20.8	50
Costa Rica	0	0	110
Dominica	0	0	10
El Salvador	95	95	125
France	4	4	4
Greece	0	0	?
Guatemala	0	2	15
Iceland	41	45	110
Indonesia	32	142	379
Italy	459	545	885
Japan	215	215	457
Kenya	45	45	105
Mexico	425	700	950
New Zealand	167	283	300
Nicaragua	35	35	?
Philippines	891	891	2,146
Portugal (Azores)	3	3	?
St. Lucia	0	0	10
Thailand	0	0.3	3
Turkey	21	21	40
United States	1,444	2,770	3,170
Former USSR	11	11	81
Totals	3,888	5,827	8,968

(Adapted and reprinted with permission from David Anderson and GRC Bulletin.)

from the fields. Despite being the world's largest source, however, this site is not typical of the geothermal energy currently used around the globe. As mentioned earlier, The Geysers is a reservoir with dry steam, whereas most of the world's geothermal resources are hot-water fields.

At its peak in 1987, The Geysers generated 1.3 million megawatts of electricity, enough for 1.3 million people. Production has slowed somewhat since the mid-1980s, however. PG&E estimates that this may drop to as low as 600 megawatts, by the year 2000. It is generally believed that this decline in production indicates that the field is fully developed. Nevertheless, performance studies have suggested that the continued life of the field is still more than fifty years. The decline of power production at The Geysers is not unique: a decline in production at dry steam fields in Italy and New Zealand has also occurred.

Experts are currently considering solutions to the gradual decrease in energy production at The Geysers. Possible techniques include reinjecting the steam back into the fields as is done already at hot-water fields, improving the efficiency at the fields, or abandoning less efficient plants in favor of more efficient ones. Water injection tests have been conducted that have arrested the decline in production in the wells, and in which some wells even showed an increase in steam flow. Although such injection is not expected to dramatically improve output in the short term, it is believed to have good potential for recovering additional heat from the reservoir rock over time.

Hawaii

Hawaii is another site of significant geothermal potential in the United States. The state has planned for the eventual production of 500 megawatts of electric power from geothermal sources, but this plan may need to be modified or halted altogether because of battles raging over the proposed geothermal development.

The concern is that geothermal development will harm much of the Wao Kele O Puna rain forest, the only lowland tropical rain forest left in the United States. Local and national environmental groups are calling the project unnecessary and unsafe. They cite both the importance of our ever-decreasing rain forests and the uncertainty of drilling just a few miles away from an active volcano.

The rain forests in Hawaii have long been home to rare species of forest birds, many of which have already become extinct or are now in danger of extinction. Further harm to these rain forests, adding to the already massive destruction of much of Hawaii's native forest, is considered unacceptable by many. Additional arguments revolve around the underwater cabling needed to transfer the generated power from its source on the Big Island of Hawaii to where it is largely needed, in Honolulu on Oahu, more than 200 miles away. The cabling would be very expensive and is technically untested.

Those in favor of geothermal development in Hawaii say that it will not harm the environment there. The Geothermal Education Office has stated that such development will not harm the state's rain forests as has happened in Brazil. In Hawaii, the office says, power plant sites, drilling sites, transmission lines, and service roads will impact on less than 1 percent of the rain forests. They do acknowledge, however, that the development would "fragment" the forests, causing problems for some plants and animals.

One of the main reasons for Hawaii's initial decision to develop its geothermal energy was a wish to become energy-independent. Hawaii currently relies on foreign oil to generate 87 percent of its electricity. Here lies the irony: that groups on either side of this issue are concerned about the environment. Those who believe that the integrity of the Hawaiian rain forests is essential are in conflict with those who wish to lessen the state's dependence on polluting fossil fuels. The eventual outcome of this situation may well be significant for future development, not only of geothermal sites, but of other renewable energy sources that run into similar difficulties.

International

The Philippines, where more than 20 percent of all power is generated from geothermal sources, and Mexico follow the United States in geothermal production. Italy, Japan, New Zealand, and China are among the other nations with current geothermal projects. Countries with good prospects for geothermal power generation by the year 2000 include Bolivia, Canada, Chile, Ethiopia, Guatemala, India, and Thailand.

Developing countries are showing a strong interest in their geothermal resources. In particular, those without indigenous fossil fuels consider geothermal development, along with other renewable sources, to be a step toward national security and energy independence. A World Bank study based on a compilation of the energy programs reported by developing countries notes that plans in these countries call for an increase in geothermal power production from two gigawatts to five gigawatts in the 1990's. Such planned increases, while not enormous, show the intention to develop this renewable energy source.

Iceland depends heavily on its geothermal resources. More than one-third of the energy consumed in that country is provided by geothermal energy. Not only is that figure unique, but the use of geothermal energy in Iceland is different from the applications in many other countries: Iceland mainly uses this type of energy for space heating. Its vast supply of low-temperature geothermal fields is tapped to provide space heating for about 85 percent of all residences and most commercial and industrial buildings. There are numerous low-temperature geothermal areas all across Iceland, with reservoir temperatures of less than 302 degrees Fahrenheit.

In addition to geothermal resources for space heating, there is much potential in Iceland for geothermal electrical power. It is estimated that there is enough geothermal energy to provide continuous electrical power on the order of 2,300 megawatts. Only a small amount has been developed thus far.

One of the earliest uses of geothermal energy, that of spas and mineral springs, is still common in many countries. In Czechoslovakia, for example, more than 2,000 mineral and thermal springs have been identified. The water from these springs varies in its chemical makeup, lending itself to a variety of uses, mainly in spas and for bottled water. There are more than sixty spa resorts throughout the country, patronized by 460,000 visitors annually. In addition, about 360 million bottles of mineral water are produced annually.

Japan is the largest user of direct geothermal heat worldwide. That country's applications include aquaculture, greenhouse heating, district heating, agricultural uses, and many industrial processes.

While many countries begin to exploit geothermal energy, some are choosing to forego this energy source in favor of other alternatives. Great Britain is one such country. Citing technical problems and high projected costs, the British government virtually halted further R&D into geothermal energy in 1991 by scaling down its program dramatically, despite the fact that Great Britain is considered to have advanced the farthest of any as far as research is concerned. There is theoretically enough geothermal energy in Cornwall alone (the focus of British research to date) to supply most of southern England's electricity needs.

□ THE FUTURE

It has been estimated that the energy equivalent of 90,000 Prudhoe Bay oil fields lies beneath the United States—just 5 percent of which would supply the country's needs for decades. While geothermal currently ranks third among alternative energy sources in use in this country, it is believed to offer the largest potential of any energy source currently available: it has been estimated that geothermal energy constitutes approximately 39 percent of this nation's total resource base of energy. (The resource base of energy includes sources not yet developed or identified specifically.)

Of the four forms of geothermal energy, only hydrothermal energy is commercially available today. The others are in various stages of development and require further research before they will be economically competitive with other energy forms, renewable or traditional. The potential for these undeveloped resources is considered by some to be even more significant than that for the hydrothermal sources we have already tapped. Geopressured resources are an example: while the U.S. Geological Survey has estimated that hydrothermal resources have an energy potential equal to approximately 23,000 megawatts over thirty years, geopressured resources over the same time period are estimated at 23,000 to 240,000 megawatts. Furthermore, the amount of energy recoverable from known magma resources has been estimated at 2,000 times the world energy demand.

In the immediate future the continued growth of a market for direct heat applications seems excellent. It has been estimated that by 2010 one application alone, vertical closed-loop pumps, will have captured 15 percent of the air-source heat pump market. We have also seen how many other applications such as aquaculture and greenhouses are becoming more popular.

There are many sites for future development. The Louisiana and Texas coasts are considered superb potential sources of geopressured energy. Sites in northern California and Hawaii have also been discussed. The Bonneville Power Administration in the Northwest is looking into developing geothermal energy in that region. In addition to the United States, the twenty countries mentioned earlier already use geothermal energy and are looking into the development of their geothermal resources. Another thirty-five countries have power plants either under construction or in the advanced planning stage, exploration programs under way or planned, or appear to hold promise for geothermal development.

Careful management of geothermal resources is very important because this energy source is not, strictly speaking, renewable—at least not on a human time scale. The Geysers field, and others in Italy and New Zealand, already offer evidence of depletion. Further research is also needed to identify the impact, if any, of the extraction of this energy source from the earth.

Another unanswered problem is what to do when the location of geothermal resources comes into conflict with existing laws and restrictions. The case in Hawaii illustrates this problem. The conflict between the need to develop alternative energy and the need to preserve precious land and natural resources comes to the fore in such situations. Many believe that the potential problems of geothermal energy extraction, namely, land subsidence and the disposal of hazardous drilling fluids, are not fully understood, and that this energy source should not be developed until the ramifications of such work are clearer. Others think that the very real dangers posed by our current energy exploitation habits provide ample reason to continue geothermal development.

☐ COSTS

In the United States, approximately 2,800 megawatts of geothermal energy are being produced at an average cost of $0.04 to $0.06 per kilowatt hour in baseload mode. An interlaboratory white paper produced for the U.S. Department of Energy in 1990 called geothermal energy "a regionally significant, currently economical renewable energy technology." Likewise, the California Public Utilities Commission, in a December 1989 report, stated that it found dry steam, flashed, and binary geothermal energy systems very cost-competitive. It also noted the economic benefit of quick order and construction times (from six months to one year) for small-scale geothermal facilities.

As has been shown with many alternative energy sources, much of the cost involved with geothermal energy is incurred at the outset. The research, drilling, and setup of the plant account for a substantial portion of the overall cost, with relatively low operating costs thereafter.

The Klamath Falls, Oregon, district heating program was initially established as a field experiment. Cost studies of this development have demonstrated that district heating costs are largely up-front, capital costs (94 percent). This system was seen to break even after five years, with a payback period of under eight years. During a study period from 1984 to 1985, geothermal energy use in this system cost two-thirds the price of natural gas.

One study showed that the cost of the average (7,200 feet deep) geothermal well in the United States is approximately $2 million in 1987 dollars, as compared with approximately $750,000 for a similar-depth onshore oil and gas well. The high costs are attributed to such factors as high temperatures, corrosive fluids, the need for larger-diameter wells, and generally more difficulty drilling in harder surfaces. There is some hope of bringing these costs down, however: other studies have shown that between 20 and 50 percent of the drilling costs could be reduced if more attention was paid to detail and with the application of the most up-to-date technology.

Development costs vary significantly from site to site. The location of the resource and its proximity to the ultimate energy consumer are important considerations. With hydrothermal energy, the generation is completed at the site and can be transferred through a grid. But direct heating systems lose heat as the heat travels farther from its source and the project cost rises as more pipe is used, so the cost advantage of a particular source can diminish greatly the farther the energy consumers are located from the energy source. The depth of the geothermal resource is another key factor in the cost. The deeper the source, the more drilling and piping needed, clearly at a higher cost.

As with other renewable energy sources, there are a variety of ways to encourage the development of geothermal energy. Making it cost-competitive is essential. The establishment, or maintenance, of financial incentives and the use of government funding are two ways to expedite this process. In the United States, a geothermal tax credit had been encouraging development of this source, but it expired in 1991 and has not been renewed. Those in the field think it is very important to reinstate this credit, develop further financial incentives, and increase the level of government funding (budgeted at $27.5 million for the 1991 fiscal year).

☐ ENVIRONMENTAL ISSUES

When it comes to the development of geothermal power, environmentalists and alternative energy supporters—people who usually work together—find themselves on opposing sides of the issue. (Nor do they see eye-to-eye on some uses of hydropower.) There are those on both sides of this issue who can cite environmental reasons for or against geothermal development. Arguments on the plus side include low emissions and little land use; on the negative side, water pollution, thermal pollution, land subsidence and sink holes, and conflicts with other environmental causes.

Geothermal energy emissions contribute less to greenhouse gases than do those from the burning of fossil fuels. The table below shows how geothermal emissions compare with those of natural gas, number-six fuel oil, and bituminous coal. (It should be noted, too, that the technology exists that can eliminate all emissions from geothermal power plants.)

Another environmental benefit of this energy source is that geothermal power plants require very little land space. In comparison with coal and other alternative energy sources, geothermal uses significantly less land, as can be seen from the table on page 96.

As noted, problems cited in making the case against the development of geothermal energy include water pollution, thermal pollution, and land subsidence and sinkholes. Most of these are considered relatively minor in comparison with alternative energy development, however, and most can also be mitigated with care and the proper technology.

Water pollution can be avoided by collecting any discharged liquids from the geothermal plant. These liquids can be disposed of by reinjection into the ground or by sending them to specially designed evaporation ponds. Care must be taken, however, if the discharged liquids are highly saline or toxic. Reinjection into the ground offers the advantage of recharging the system and the prevention of land subsidence. If the liquids are to be discharged into ponds, they may need to be treated to prevent contamination of surface- and groundwaters.

Thermal pollution from a geothermal plant is two to three times worse at the plant site than at a nuclear plant. However, it has been pointed out that this initial disadvantage is offset by the thermal pollution created from the mining, processing, fabrication, transportation, and reprocessing of the nuclear fuel.

The problem of land subsidence and sink holes has been seen at a

ENERGY SOURCE	EMISSIONS[a]
Geothermal[b]	0.3
Natural gas	282.0
Number–six fuel oil	418.0
Bituminous coal	497.0

a. Emissions measured in pounds of carbon per megawatt hour of electricity generated.

b. The newest generation of geothermal power plants.

(Source: Earth Science Laboratory, University of Utah Research Institute (UURI), "Geothermal Energy.")

Technology	Land occupied[a]
Coal[b]	3,642
Solar thermal	3,561
Photovoltaics	3,237
Wind[c]	1,335
Geothermal	404

a. Land is measured in square meters per gigawatt hour, over thirty years.
b. Includes coal mining.
c. Land actually occupied by turbines and service roads.

(Reprinted with permission from Worldwatch Institute.)

power plant in Wairekei, New Zealand, where a depression covering 24 square miles has developed. While reinjection of the geothermal fluids is being carried out to minimize subsidence, its effects are still under observation. It should be noted that most geothermal technologies integrate reinjection into their design.

All things considered, it does look as though geothermal energy will be developed in the future, for it is generally believed that the environmental benefits outweigh any drawbacks. The only exception would be in instances in which geothermal development comes into conflict with other environmental concerns, as is the case in Hawaii.

☐ BENEFITS AND CONCERNS

The environmental benefits discussed in the preceding section—lower air emissions, limited land use, and the avoidance of fossil fuels—are clear advantages associated with geothermal energy. Energy conservation is another plus. As in the case of geothermal heat pumps, using geothermal resources can significantly cut energy consumption.

Other advantages to geothermal energy include its reliability and availability. Once a geothermal resource is found and established, it provides energy on a regular basis; unlike some other energy sources, it is not affected by weather or seasonal changes. At existing geothermal power plants, availability is 95 percent, as compared with less than 80 percent at the average fossil fuel plant and less than 70 percent at nuclear plants.

Shorter lead times and construction periods for geothermal plants in comparison with traditional power plants can also be an advantage. Cost can be an advantage, too, depending on the specific site and its intended use.

Countries that develop a domestic geothermal resource can reduce their reliance on foreign energy supplies. Energy security and improved trade balances are direct benefits from such an energy strategy.

Geothermal resources may eventually provide arid or drought-stricken areas with sources of fresh water, also. Particularly liquid-dominated resources can provide the water and the inexpensive energy to purify it. Even heavily salinated liquids can be purified to provide potable water.

The greatest disadvantage of geothermal energy occurs in situations when its development conflicts with other environmental concerns. High up-front costs, including exploration, assessment, and drilling, can also be a disadvantage, depending on the site. Financing that takes into consideration the long-term view could help overcome this problem, but this is not always available.

To sum up: geothermal energy represents a vast potential resource, both in the United States and worldwide. It can be used in a variety of ways: to create electricity, to provide direct heat, and to create mechanical energy. Although only one of its four energy forms, hydrothermal energy, is currently being exploited, its electrical and direct heat applications have proven themselves technically reliable and economically competitive. Researchers believe that it will not be long before geopressured and hot dry rock sources will also be available at competitive prices. While there are still some technical problems to be solved regarding the undeveloped resources, and some environmental conflicts over hydrothermal development in specific instances, it appears that geothermal energy will play an important role in providing energy for the world in the future.

5

BIOMASS ENERGY

Biomass includes any organic plant or animal matter. Biomass energy, or bioenergy, is a general term that encompasses the energy stored in these organic wastes, its conversion into useful energy, and the ultimate use of that energy. Conversion of these materials to energy can be as simple as cutting trees and burning them or as complex as taking sugarcane or other crops and converting their sugars into liquid fuels. The beauty of biomass energy production is that conversion technologies can replace a wide variety of traditional energy sources. Biomass energy can replace fossil fuels in solid or liquid forms, and can generate both electricity and direct heat.

The most common sources of biomass energy are wood and wood wastes, but there are numerous additional sources. These include agricultural residues, animal wastes, municipal solid waste (MSW), and microalgae and other aquatic plants. Crops can also be grown with the express purpose of harvesting their energy content.

An important point to make with biomass technology is that the carbon inherent in the organic matter is recycled. Unlike the burning of fossil fuels, combustion of biomass simply recycles the carbon fixed by photosynthesis in the growth phase. This accounts for the relative lack of air pollution inherent in biomass energy production. Simply put, the combustion of plant matter releases no more carbon dioxide than is absorbed by its growth, so the net contribution to greenhouse gases is zero.

Wood and wood wastes encompass a variety of components, including both residues from the forest and residues from the mill. For example, unsalable trees and logging slash (branches and the tops of trees) can be used as biomass fuel. At the mill, bark, sawdust, and other mill wastes serve as potential fuel. Agricultural residues might include corncobs, sugarcane bagasse (the residue stalk after the juice has been extracted), leaves, and rice hulls. MSW provides a large supply of potential biomass energy, too. Paper, cloth, yard wastes, miscellaneous construction debris, and packaging materials are just a few of the materials with potential energy found in our solid waste. Medium-BTU gas is already being collected at more than 120 landfills in the United States. Finally, energy crops include grains, algae and other water plants, grasses, and oil-bearing plants. (See accompanying list.)

Of course, the biomass materials used in any particular country or region vary depending on local resources. In the Caribbean and other tropical climates, for example, sugarcane is widely grown and so bagasse is a common biomass energy feedstock. Rice-growing countries use rice husks; the Midwest of the United States uses corn husks; and heavily forested areas use timber residues.

Biomass energy feedstocks can be generated in two ways: by using actual agricultural, industrial, or municipal wastes or by growing plants specifically for energy production. The former method increases the efficiency of existing activities, whereas the latter requires the infrastructure of an entire agricultural system. In the latter case, the use of what have become known as "energy farms" raises some concerns about competing with agricultural land for food and the increased use of pesticides. Nevertheless, energy farms have the potential of providing an important energy resource.

It is important to note that biomass is not a renewable resource unless creation of the source exceeds its use. This applies both to energy farms and to standard crops, particularly forests. For example, some countries are using fast-rotation trees for energy. This policy cannot be considered renewable energy unless at least the same number of trees are replanted as have been harvested for energy production. Sustainability is essential if this energy source is to be used responsibly.

☐ HISTORY OF BIOMASS ENERGY

Human beings have always relied heavily on biomass energy. Before the use of coal and other sources became more widespread, biomass (mainly in the form of firewood) was the principal energy source in the United States. This was also the case in other countries: in Canada, for example, at the time of its confederation in 1867, biomass was almost the exclusive energy source, with only 10 percent of the new nation's energy supply coming from other sources such as coal and hydropower.

During the twentieth century, first coal, and then oil, became more prevalent and the importance of biomass lessened, reaching its low near 1960. Since that date, the trend has begun to reverse itself, and biomass is once again gaining popularity as an energy source. The forest products industry worldwide now supplies a large percentage of its own energy needs (between 65 and 100 percent, depending on the country) by using

SAMPLE SOURCES OF BIOMASS

WOOD AND WOOD WASTES

Trees (eucalyptus, poplar, firs, pines, lucaena, locusts, willows, sycamore, red alder, elms, maples)

Shrubs (chaparral, mesquite)

Forest residue (logging residue, clearing, removal)

Mill residue (bark, sawdust, coarse residue)

OTHER WASTES

MSW (paper, food and yard wastes, plastics, wood, tires)

Livestock waste (manure)

Process waste (industrial, food processing)

Sewage (sludge)

AGRICULTURAL CROPS AND RESIDUES

Crop residues (cane tops, straw, husks, citrus peels, corn stalks)

Cotton gin trash

Bagasse (sugarcane pulp)

Molasses

Starch crops (corn, wheat, sorghum, barley)

Sugar crops (cane, beet, sorghum)

Forage crops (alfalfa, grasses, fescue, clover)

Oilseed crops (soybean, sunflower, safflower)

SALT- AND FRESHWATER AQUATIC PLANTS

Algae (kelp, oil-producing microalgae, spirulina)

Water weed

Water hyacinth

Reeds and rushes

UNCONVENTIONAL CROPS

Arid land plants (guayule, rabbit brush, goldenrod, creosote bush, sassafras, gopher plant, milkweed)

Saline plants (salt bush, reed grass, seepwood, Russian thistle, greasewood)

(Adapted and reprinted with permission from the Western Area Power Administration.)

wood scraps for fuel. Likewise, home heating with firewood has regained popularity, and even utilities have begun to provide some of their energy through wood-burning plants.

As with renewable energy in general, some of the increased interest in biomass can be traced to the oil embargo in the 1970s. During the same decade, the United States passed the Clean Water Act (1972) and the Clean Air Act (1970), both of which forced industry to look at energy sources that produced fewer pollutants.

□ THE TECHNOLOGY

Plants create energy through photosynthesis, retaining solar radiation and converting carbon dioxide and water into energy products. We can then take that energy and transform it through a variety of processes to make it suitable to our uses. There are three basic types of bioenergy conversion used today: direct combustion, thermochemical conversion, and biochemical conversion.

Direct Combustion

Direct combustion of wood and other plant matter has always been a primary energy source for human beings. This particular type of biomass energy conversion is both the oldest and the most widely used today, largely because almost any type of biomass can be burned to produce heat, steam, or electricity.

Today, the technology for power plants using direct combustion of wood, wood waste, or MSW is well-developed. Direct combustion systems vary largely in size. Large power plants may produce up to 400 megawatts of energy, whereas smaller systems include those used for space heating and home wood-burning stoves. Most direct combustion systems can take any type of biomass as long as its moisture content is less than 60 percent. While wood and wood residues are most commonly used, a variety of other agricultural residues can also be used as feedstock.

Thermochemical Conversion

Thermochemical conversion processes use heat in an oxygen-free or oxygen-deficient environment to produce chemical changes in biomass. The process can produce electricity, gas, oil, char, heat, methanol, and other products. Gasification, pyrolysis, and liquefaction are all thermochemical methods of converting biomass into energy. Any one of these processes may be used, depending on the end products desired.

Gasification

Gasification is a partial-combustion process used to turn biomass into a mixture of gases. Gasification processes can be direct or indirect. The former uses air or heat to produce partial combustion in a reactor; the latter transfers heat to a reactor from outside through its walls using heat exchangers or hot sand.

This process produces low- or medium–BTU gases from wood and wood wastes, agricultural residues, and MSW which can be used on their own or as feedstock for other products. For example, processing these synthetic gases with water can produce ammonia, methanol, or hydrogen. The resultant gases can be burned in a furnace (direct heat gasification) or in an internal combustion engine.

Commercial gasification systems exist and show good potential for future use. Their widespread use has been limited to date by hauling distances for the feedstock, however.

Pyrolysis

Pyrolysis, a type of gasification, breaks down biomass, again in oxygen-deficient environments, at temperatures of up to 400 degrees Fahrenheit. This process has traditionally been used to produce charcoal.

Because the temperatures used in this process are lower than those in other gasification methods, the end products are different. The slow heating produces roughly equal proportions of gas, liquid, and charcoal, but the output can be varied by changing the input, the temperature, and the time in the reactor. The gases produced consist of carbon monoxide, hydrogen, carbon dioxide, and smaller amounts of methane, ethane, and other hydrocarbons. The solids are carbon and ash. The liquids that result are similar to crude oil and usually must be treated before they can be used as liquid fuels.

Liquefaction

In liquefaction systems, wood and wood wastes are primarily used. These are reacted with steam or hydrogen and carbon monoxide to produce liquids and chemicals. The chemical reactions that take place in this process are basically the same as for gasification but at lower temperatures and higher pressure. Liquefaction processes can be either direct or indirect.

The end product from liquefaction is pyrolytic oil, an oil with a high oxygen content. Pyrolytic oil requires extensive refining to be used for anything other than direct combustion. Depending on the process used, it can be converted to either a diesel fuel, a gasoline, or methanol.

Biochemical Conversion

Biochemical conversion, or bioconversion, is a chemical reaction caused by treating particularly moist biomass with microorganisms such as enzymes or fungi. The end products can be either liquid or gaseous fuels. Anaerobic digestion and fermentation are the two processes used for biochemically converting biomass to energy.

Anaerobic Digestion
As its name suggests, this conversion process takes place without air. The feedstock, moist biomass such as sewage sludge, MSW, animal waste, kelp, algae, or agricultural waste, is placed in a reaction vessel with bacteria. The bacteria break down the biomass and create a gas that is 50 to 60 percent methane. This gas can be used in several ways: to produce space heat, process heat or steam; in an engine to produce mechanical or electrical energy (the most common use in the United States); or purified to operate through a natural gas system.

The use of anaerobic digestion systems is widespread. Small-scale digesters have been used on Asian and European farms for centuries; sewage treatment plants have used this process for years to generate methane; and communities across the United States use digesters to compost municipal organic waste, making a valuable mulch as the end product. Anaerobic systems can vary greatly in size, from large industrial systems that handle 400,000 cubic feet of material and produce 1.5 million cubic feet of biogas per day to small farm systems that handle 400 cubic feet of material and produce 6,000 cubic feet of biogas per day.

Fermentation
We have known for centuries that fermenting grains with yeast produces a grain alcohol. The process also works with certain other biomass materials. In fermentation, the yeast decomposes carbohydrates (starches, in the case of grains, or sugar from sugarcane juice) into ethyl alcohol (ethanol) and carbon dioxide (a valuable by-product in its own right). The process breaks down complex substances into simple ones. Fermentation using bacteria produces pharmaceutical products. Fermentable sugars can be obtained directly from certain plants, like sugarcane or beets, or by processing cellulose-based materials such as wood, straw, or pretreated agricultural wastes.

Fuel ethanol is a growing industry in the United States and around the world, offering an alternative to traditional gasoline as an automobile fuel. Brazil has the largest ethanol industry, producing almost three billion gallons each year from sugarcane. Ethanol and other alternative fuels are discussed in more detail in the following chapter.

□ CURRENT STATUS

The application of biomass energy worldwide is well established. Biomass is used not out of concern for the environment, but rather for survival: approximately 2.5 billion people (about one-half of the world's population) rely on biomass for almost all their cooking, heating, and lighting needs. The use of biomass is widespread, diverse, and geared to the specific feedstock available locally. Forest and agricultural lands, arid lands, marshlands, and fresh and coastal waters can all provide excellent biomass resources.

Developed and lesser-developed countries alike can profit from the use of this natural resource, although to date the latter utilize biomass resources much more than do the former. Biomass accounts for approximately 12 or 13 percent of overall energy production worldwide, whereas in developing countries that amount can be as high as 50 percent. (Of course, some developed countries rely heavily on biomass, but this is the exception, not the rule.) The most widespread use of biomass for energy is in the rural areas of developing nations. Researchers have pointed out the extent to which certain nations depend on biomass. For example, Nepal, Ethiopia, and Haiti derive most of their energy from biomass; Kenya, Maldives, India, Indonesia, Sri Lanka, and Mauritius derive over half; China, Papua New Guinea, Samoa, and Cape Verde over one-third; Brazil one-quarter; and Egypt and Morocco one-fifth.

Although Brazil's program is discussed in further detail in the next chapter, it is worth noting here that this country has an extensive fuel alcohol program, the largest in the world. Brazil produces fuel alcohol from sugar and starch crops, and the government spends approximately $1.3 billion yearly to subsidize this industry.

In the United States, approximately 5 to 8 percent of the energy consumed is provided by biomass. Of that, it is estimated that 90 percent comes from direct combustion of wood and wood residues. The use of biomass has increased over the past decade from an installed capacity of 200 megawatts in 1980 to more than 7,700 megawatts in 1990. Biomass accounts for 50 percent of the total amount of renewable energy currently produced in this country.

The search for cleaner fuels and growing landfill restraints are among the reasons for the increase in biomass utilization. About half of Americans live in areas that exceed national ambient air quality standards (NAAQS) for ozone. The cost of waste disposal has escalated, and landfill sites are closing much faster than new ones are opening. In fact, the Environmental Protection Agency (EPA) has estimated that between 1978 and 1988, 70 percent of the nation's landfills, approximately 14,000 facilities, closed. It projects that by 1995 half of the remaining sites will have closed as well.

Some states have developed biomass energy production more than others. In Florida, power plants generate more than 700 megawatts of energy from biomass, and 23 percent of Maine's baseload requirements are met with biomass electrical facilities. (Maine leads all other states in this aspect.) Hawaii generates about one-half of its energy from renewable sources, and biomass provides about 50 percent of that. Certain states are prime candidates for specific biomass utilization. For example, the five states that use the highest amount of wood and wood waste for industrial/commercial purposes are Georgia, Alabama, Louisiana, Mississippi, and North Carolina—all densely forested states. Likewise, states with high populations are using biomass to solve some of their waste problems. Florida, California, and New York are among the largest users of MSW for energy.

In Canada, biomass represents a growing contributor to the national energy supply. In 1990 biomass energy equaled the energy produced by the nuclear industry and represented approximately one-half of that produced from coal. Some regions use biomass to a much greater degree: biomass accounts for 12 percent of the energy supply in the Atlantic region and 23 percent in British Columbia. The use of biomass energy in Canada is spreading to a number of sectors, including greenhouse heating, health-care facilities, educational institutions, office and apartment buildings, and large industrial applications like automobile manufacturing and food processing.

Other developed nations that generate higher proportions of their energy needs from biomass include Ireland (17 percent) and Sweden (13 percent).

□ APPLICATIONS

Because biomass can generate energy in many different forms (including gases, heat, steam, electricity, and feedstocks for the chemical industry, these resources are applicable to a variety of end uses. Biomass resources serve as solid fuel for direct burning, as is the case with refuse-derived fuels (such as from MSW) that produce steam or electric power. They can equally be converted to other fuel forms through chemical or biological processes, as in the case of ethanol or methanol fuels. The vast majority of the energy generated from biomass comes from direct combustion technologies, with wood and wood wastes being the most common feedstock. (See accompanying table.)

In the United States wood energy is used in all fifty states and produces electricity in forty-two states. Industrial, commercial, and utility applications account for approximately two-thirds of the wood used for energy. For example, the wood and pulp industries use their wastes to provide a significant proportion of their own heat, steam, and electricity needs. Likewise, utilities, particularly in California, have wood-burning

Utilization of the Biomass Resource in the United States

Wood and wood waste (industrial/commercial)	51%
Wood (residential space heating)	34%
MSW, agricultural wastes, landfill gas and biogas, alcohol fuels	15%

(Source: Rader, "The Power of the States," p. 6)

power plants that feed into the electrical grid system. Large industrial companies such as Dow Corning and Proctor and Gamble also use biomass energy. Residential heating and district heating are still other applications.

Urban wood—the residue from construction sites and building demolitions—is becoming a more popular source of energy. In California, particularly, more than 800 megawatts of biomass capacity have been added since 1980 to accommodate the increased utilization of urban and standard wood residues.

Wood is not the only biomass feedstock that can be burned directly. In Hawaii, the sugar industry produces at least 150 megawatts of energy from burning bagasse. Nearly half of the energy produced is sold to local electrical utilities. Worldwide, agricultural by-products are often used on-site to produce heat and electricity for farm buildings.

Mills that process rice can also generate process heat. This can be used for direct heat, steam generation, mechanical power, and electrical power. The amount of energy available can be significant: for every five tons of rice milled, one ton of husks with an energy content roughly similar to one ton of wood remains as residue. One rice mill in Louisiana has received all its power needs since 1984 from an on-site rice-husk power plant. The plant generates surplus energy and sells the remaining electricity to the local utility grid.

Of course, other organic matter—not just plants—can be used as an energy feedstock. The first commercial power plant to burn cattle manure to generate electricity was established in the Imperial Valley of southern California in 1987. This plant has a capacity of about seventeen megawatts and supplies electricity to 20,000 homes. The manure is burned to produce steam, which drives a generator and produces the electricity. Biomass feedstocks can also be used to create gaseous and liquid fuels. These can be used on-site, to improve the efficiency of the processing system in question, or they can be transported off-site in a suitable form to be used in other applications. Some of these qualifications include direct sale to utilities, thermal energy, motor fuels, or chemical feedstocks.

Sugar, starch, or lignocellulosic biomass (such as wood, energy crops, or MSW) can produce alcohols such as methanol, ethanol, and butanol. A major application of these fuels is as a substitute, or additive, to conventional automobile gasoline. Microalgae and oilseed crops also produce diesel fuel. The use of these alcohol fuels can reduce air pollution. There are additional applications for these alcohols. Methane created from anaerobically digested manure was used to light streets in England as early as 1895. Anaerobic digestion also produces high-quality fertilizers.

☐ BENEFITS AND CONCERNS

The benefits of developing biomass energy are numerous. These include economic, political, social, and environmental advantages.

One of the strongest arguments in favor of biomass development is the enormous potential of the resource base. The energy potential of biomass has been estimated at approximately forty-two quadrillion BTUs—more than half of the total current energy consumption in the United States. This energy source already provides the nation with the same amount of energy as the nuclear industry, but without the hazards.

Biomass is accessible immediately. There is no need for years of further development as can be the case with some other alternative energy options. Another advantage is its diversity, both in the kind of energy produced and in its resource base. Biomass can provide substitutes for fossil fuels (liquid, gaseous, or solid) as well as electricity and heat. Its resource base is well spread out and varied. Arid land, wetlands, forest, and agricultural lands can all provide a variety of plants and organic matter to be used as biomass feedstock.

Biomass production can offer many economic advantages. It can increase the profitability of the industries involved and decrease the costs of power generation. For example, facilities can convert waste products (wood chips, bagasse, etc.) to energy for on-site use instead of throwing away the waste, thus lowering disposal costs and saving the costs of buying some or all of their energy supplies from outside sources. Likewise, profitability can increase if an industry uses its waste to create energy. In the sugar industry, for example, converting bagasse to energy means that a facility not only has sugar to sell, but energy also—not to mention decreased disposal costs. A further advantage is that biomass facilities often require less construction time, capital, and financing than larger, conventional plants.

Likewise, biomass production can provide increased employment in rural areas through the cultivation and processing of the feedstocks. In the Northeast alone, biomass accounts for $1.2 billion in the regional economy and 80,000 jobs. Biomass production offers crop alternatives and the potential for increased income to farmers. Fields that are not used in winter can produce biomass, and varying crops in the same fields can help protect soil quality.

The very fact that biomass consists largely (to date) of waste materials has significant implications for one of society's more pressing problems—waste disposal. The decrease in both landfill volume and general pollution that results from biomass energy production is certainly beneficial to society.

Politically, biomass energy offers the nation that develops this natural resource several benefits. Decreased dependence on imported fossil fuels (and the consequential decreased outflow of capital and foreign dependence) and increased self-sufficiency and energy security are important for any nation. Of course, it shares these benefits with other indigenous renewable sources.

The environmental benefits to biomass energy production are clearly important, too. Scott Sklar of the National Wood Energy Association puts it quite succinctly: "Biomass energy offers what no other conventional fuel offers—increased supply with a positive environmental impact." Biomass energy production does not cause acid rain because it contains little sulfur and nitrogen. If grown on a sustainable basis, it causes no net increase in carbon dioxide (the chief cause of greenhouse gases), and the use of alcohol fuels reduces carbon monoxide emissions.

Finally, biomass is renewable—as long as it is grown on a sustainable basis. By using biomass as an energy source, we are not depleting valuable natural resources.

Of course, there are two sides to every issue. The concerns about the development of biomass energy include practical and economic issues, but are mainly of an environmental nature.

Some practical concerns relate to the bulkiness of certain biomass resources. Although these resources are widespread, they must be used locally since their bulk makes it expensive to transport the feedstocks very far. In California, for example, it is uneconomical to transport wood residues farther than 100 miles. The bulkiness of biomass resources can also cause storage problems. Other practical concerns relate to the efficiency of and available technology for biomass resources. Many biomass feedstocks have a high moisture content, which lowers their heat value. Preprocessing can help this problem, however. Further, while there are many biomass conversion technologies available and in use today, concerns exist that some of these are still only marginally beneficial economically or technically, keeping them from being cost-competitive in certain situations.

The environmental concerns revolve around the possible effects of irresponsibly managed, nonsustainable biomass development. An uncontrolled increase in biomass energy production has the potential to cause serious environmental problems. Land-use issues and concerns about increased pollution are chief among observers' concerns.

As far as land use is concerned, many fear that biomass developers will give in to the temptation to deplete our forests, not replanting as many trees as are harvested, or to target old-growth forests. Concerns also exist that already-rare wetlands, which house fragile ecosystems and rare species, might be used rather than preserved. On agricultural lands, critics are wary of competition with food production. The loss of soil fertility from overuse is also a concern. To avoid these potential land-use problems, biomass energy production must be varied and sustainable, being careful to preserve local ecosystems.

Pollution problems from biomass development may not be quite so easy to solve. The increased use of fertilizers and bioengineered organisms on energy farms and the introduction of hazardous chemicals from MSW into the agricultural process, with potential resultant air and water pollution, are real issues that need to be studied.

☐ COSTS

There are two ways to look at the costs involved in biomass energy development. First, using wastes on-site can save energy costs for the production facility in question. Biomass is also generated and sold as an energy source on its own, in competition with fossil fuels in the marketplace.

While there are environmental benefits to be had from the use of biomass energy, the primary reason for installing wood or other energy systems in industries or institutions is usually to achieve a net savings in energy costs. These savings will be realized when the energy costs of the source(s) being replaced are less than the total operating and installation costs of the biomass system. Plants and factories around the world have switched to biomass—with significant savings. Greenhouses, lumber mills, canneries, farmers, and manufacturers can offset traditional energy costs and save in disposal costs by using their waste as feedstock for energy systems. One study of biomass use in Honduras showed that an energy-efficient power plant using all the wastes of a large lumber mill and selling power to the grid for at least $0.05 per kilowatt hour would produce an internal rate of return on equity investment of 75 percent, and would pay back the initial investment in just over three years. In Ireland, greenhouses raising early tomatoes are heated with biomass from willow wood. The willow wood fuel costs one-third as much as the oil it replaces.

A project by the United States Agency for International Development studied the potential of sugarcane residues for electrical grid power in various countries, including Thailand, Jamaica, the Philippines, and Costa Rica. The project noted that cane power systems have the potential to provide electric power at lower unit costs than most or all of the other power generation options available to the countries studied. In Thailand the study team found that a new cane power plant would supply power at $0.028 to $0.032 per kilowatt hour. This cost was well below the cost of power generated in that country with imported coal ($0.044 per kilowatt hour) or with domestic natural gas ($0.040 per kilowatt hour).

Utilities are also beginning to consider biomass as an energy source because of the potential economic benefits. For example, a study by the

California Energy Commission demonstrated that wood-fired boilers can be installed for approximately $1,340 per kilowatt, which is 20 percent less than a coal plant costs. Currently, the cost for utility-connected electricity from biomass energy is approximately $0.06 per kilowatt hour.

The potential lower price of biomass energy is related to the installation and development of biomass conversion plants. As shown earlier, these plants, which are often smaller than their fossil fuel counterparts, can be built more quickly, less expensively, and with less capital investment. These considerations obviously have a positive effect on the final price of biomass energy.

Biomass wastes are being used more frequently across the United States and around the world, offering a cost-effective energy alternative. Energy plants (those grown specifically for energy production), however, are not currently cost-competitive with fossil fuels. New biotechnologies are being developed to improve energy production in crops, and new combustion technologies and more efficient gas turbines are expected to increase the efficiency, thereby lowering the cost, of biomass energy production overall.

☐ THE FUTURE

The future looks promising for biomass energy. Experts believe that over the next decade the contribution of biomass fuels to U.S. energy supply could increase three- or fourfold, providing 15 to 20 percent of our energy needs by the year 2000. For this to happen, government R&D funding for biomass is essential. (Such funding increased slightly in the 1990 fiscal year, but had decreased more than 75 percent from 1980 to 1989.) The U.S. Department of Energy projected in 1989 that biomass could potentially become the world's largest single energy source if intervention to protect the climate takes place.

Nations around the world are developing their indigenous biomass resources, and this trend is expected to continue. France, for example, is looking into short-rotation forestry on more than 400 hectares of land. Northern Ireland is conducting similar experiments. India is expanding its already established network of biogas digesters, which supplies compost to farmers and electricity to local communities. Finland, a nation that already provides almost 20 percent of its energy needs from biomass, is aiming to increase its energy self-sufficiency to between 32 and 35 percent through the use of forest and peat feedstocks.

Experts believe that direct combustion applications will continue to have the greatest impact in the near future because they are available today and offer environmental benefits in comparison to fossil fuels. More exotic fuels such as those derived from algae will also appear, but these still need a few more years of development time. Technological advances anticipated in certain areas will facilitate biomass energy development; these areas include microorganisms for use in anaerobic digesters, genetic engineering of superior microbes, yeasts, and fungi, catalytic processing of lignins to liquid fuels, and fermentation techniques.

One of the significant features of biomass energy production in the future is expected to be the increase in energy farms, farms that grow biomass feedstock specifically to generate energy. Increased use of MSW as a fuel is also expected. With the United States currently producing more than 200 million tons of garbage each year, our MSW offers a large, growing resource, even after recyclables are removed from the waste stream. (Note: the author advocates burning MSW only after thorough removal of recyclables and hazardous wastes.)

It has been said that it would be theoretically possible to replace the use of fossil fuels worldwide with biomass energy. While its success to this extent is unlikely, few doubt that biomass will play an important role in our energy future.

6

RENEWABLE
AUTOMOBILE FUELS

Few disagree that something must be done about our use of energy in the transportation sector. In 1988 alone, U.S. vehicles consumed more than ten million barrels of oil per day—more than 63 percent of the total U.S. consumption and 22 percent more than the amount of oil produced in the United States. This state of affairs clearly has implications not only for the environment, but also for the energy security and international trade position of the United States.

Transportation sources currently generate over two-thirds of carbon monoxide emissions in the United States. Because of the significant effect that widespread use of alternative fuels could have on our environment, the current chapter focuses on this one particular application of biomass energy. There are a number of alternative motor fuels available today. Some of these are made from renewable sources, and others are not. The focus here is on automotive fuels that are generated from renewable sources.

This is not a straightforward subject. While alternative fuels are increasing in popularity, a variety of issues remain to be resolved before we can expect to see widespread use of these new energy sources. Some of these problems are cost-related; some have to do with infrastructure; and many of the unresolved issues deal with the environmental impact of the various alternative fuels being considered today. There is still significant debate among proponents of the various fuel sources about which is the best alternative to gasoline.

The bulk of this chapter looks at the renewable methods of generating methanol and ethanol (not all methods of making these fuels use renewable resources), the two most likely competitors to gasoline at the pumps. Compressed natural gas, a fuel that is increasing in use, is also discussed.

☐ WHAT ARE RENEWABLE AUTOMOBILE FUELS?

The alternative transportation fuels currently being studied vary widely in their makeup, stage of development, and practicality. Each of these has its advantages and disadvantages when compared both with today's gasoline and with each other. Methanol, ethanol, and compressed natural gas all have their particular supporters.

Methanol

Methanol, commonly called wood alcohol, is a colorless and odorless liquid alcohol fuel that can be made from biomass, natural gas, or coal. It can be used as an automotive fuel in its pure form (M100), as a gasoline blend—usually 85 percent methane to 15 percent unleaded gasoline (M85)—or as a feedstock for reformulated gasoline, or methyl tertiary butyl ether (MTBE). In M85 the gasoline is added to give a color to the flame of the burning fuel (for safety in case of fires) and to help the vehicle start in very cold weather.

Methanol production from natural gas, coal, or biomass is technically possible today. But production must become more efficient, and a sufficient infrastructure must be developed to make it economically competitive, if methanol is to be a viable alternative fuel. Natural gas is currently the most economical source of methane, a situation expected to continue for at least another decade. Although the United States has vast quantities of both natural gas and coal (as do other nations), these are both nonrenewable resources; biomass is the only renewable feedstock for methane.

Biomass resources that can serve as feedstocks for methane production include crop residues, municipal solid waste (MSW), and wood resources. When used in a sustainable fashion, biomass provides an endless resource for the generation of methane. Estimates of biomass resources available for the production of alcohol fuels range from one million to 4.7 million dry tons per day (one ton equaling 100 gallons of methanol when biomass is also used to fuel the processing plant).

Ethanol

Ethanol, or grain alcohol, is another alcohol fuel with the potential of becoming a widely used automotive fuel. Like methanol, it can be made from a variety of feedstocks, mainly grains, forest residues, and MSW. It can also be used in its pure form or in blends, similarly to methane. Gasoline blends using 90 percent gasoline and 10 percent ethanol are widely used, and in fact approximately 7.5 percent of the gasoline sold in the United States today contains this mixture. Ethyl tertiary butyl ether (ETBE), a feedstock for reformulated gasoline based on ethanol, is being studied but as yet has seen no commercial production.

Almost all (95 percent) of the ethanol used today in the United States is made from corn. Other countries, particularly Brazil, use sugar as their main resource. Research is currently under way to improve methods for generating ethanol from agricultural and forest feedstocks and MSW; although these resources work well—in fact, ethanol can be produced more efficiently from wood sources—their development is not as advanced as that of corn or sugar, and the production of ethanol from them is much more expensive.

Compressed Natural Gas (CNG)

Natural gas is a fossil fuel that is extracted from underground reservoirs. It consists mainly of methane, with smaller amounts of other hydrocarbons such as ethane, propane, and butane, and inert gases such as carbon dioxide, nitrogen, and helium. The actual composition of the gas varies, depending on its source. To be employed as a vehicle fuel, natural gas can be used either in its compressed form (compressed natural gas, or CNG) or in its liquid form (liquefied natural gas). Discussion in this chapter focuses on CNG, currently the form most commonly used as an automotive fuel.

The same characteristic that makes CNG practical for fleet and delivery vehicles hinders its widespread use in most passenger cars: a tank can only hold enough fuel for approximately 100 miles. Until CNG filling stations are much more widespread, the distance restriction creates a severe limitation to this fuel's development.

☐ HISTORY OF RENEWABLE AUTOMOBILE FUELS

Alcohol fuels are not new. The catalytic synthesis of methanol was first commercialized in Germany in 1923. Before that, methane was made by the distillation or pyrolysis of wood, relatively inefficient processes. Ethanol has experienced several periods of temporary popularity throughout the past century, particularly during the two world wars when petroleum was scarce. In recent decades the use of these alcohol fuels has developed rapidly, both in pure and various mixed forms.

The growth in worldwide use of MTBE, in particular, has been very rapid. The first MTBE plant was built in Italy in 1973, and its use quickly spread throughout Europe. By 1979, the installed capacity in Europe was eighty-eight million gallons per year, increasing to 328 million gallons per year in 1988. In the United States MTBE production began in 1979 and had reached more than one billion gallons by 1987.

As we have seen with other renewable energy sources, the current interest in alternative automobile fuels can be traced to the oil crisis in the 1970s. It has been spurred on more recently by environmental concerns about air quality and greenhouse gases. In the United States there has been some recent legislation requiring government and industry to focus on developing cleaner-burning gasoline substitutes and gasoline enhancers and on producing more efficient automobiles. In particular, the 1988 Alternative Motor Fuels Act (AMFA) and the 1990 amendments to the Clean Air Act (of 1970) dictate the latest government policy and targets in this area. While many believe this legislation does not go nearly far enough in regulating the undesirable environmental effects from our automobiles, it is nonetheless a step forward and, for better or worse, it sets forth the goals toward which industry is now working.

The main focus of AMFA is to develop demonstration programs that will encourage the use of alternative fuels and alternative-fuel vehicles. The act also offers credits to automakers for producing alternative-fuel vehicles and incentives that encourage federal agencies to buy such vehicles.

The 1990 amendments to the Clean Air Act cover a wide range of issues. In "The New Clean Air Act: What It Means to You," the EPA lists its major provisions as follows:

■ new cars sold from 1994 on will emit about thirty percent less hydrocarbons and 60 percent less nitrogen-oxide pollutants from the tailpipe than today's cars do;

■ starting "in a few years" [quotes added], new cars will have diagnostic equipment capable of alerting the driver to malfunctioning emission-control equipment;

■ beginning on October 1, 1993, oil refiners will be required to reduce the amount of sulfur in diesel fuel;

■ beginning in the winter of 1992/93, oxygen (which reduces carbon monoxide emissions) will be added to all gasoline sold during winter months in any city with carbon monoxide problems;

■ beginning in 1996 auto companies must sell 150,000 cars in California that have emission levels one-half that allowed for other new cars. This number increases to 300,000 a year in 1999 and in 2001 the emission levels are reduced by half again;

■ beginning in 1998 a percentage of new vehicles purchased in centrally-fueled fleets in twenty-two polluted cities must meet tailpipe standards that are about one-third of those in place for general passenger cars.

□ THE TECHNOLOGY

For alternative fuels to be widely used, changes must take place both in the infrastructure of the fuel industry and in the manufacture of automobiles. Infrastructural changes will include improved availability of the alternative fuels, whichever they may be. This can be done by increasing the number of filling stations that offer them, and by establishing a distribution system that is as efficient as the current gasoline system.

Technological changes in the manufacture of automobiles may be required if they are to run on alternative fuels. Such changes may not be uniform, and in fact it is likely that society will move away from a single-fuel system to a multifuel (and hence, multivehicle, or adjustable vehicle) system.

The Automobiles

There are a variety of scenarios for the way in which automobiles may be adjusted to allow for alternative fuels. Dual-fuel, flexible-fuel, or dedicated-fuel systems, all of which are being used to some extent around the world today, are all possible options.

With a dual-fuel engine, a vehicle can operate on either gasoline or an alternative fuel. Typically, the vehicle can switch between a liquid or gaseous fuel. Cars, trucks, and buses that use both gasoline and CNG are used in northern Italy.

Flexible-fuel vehicles are designed to use a variable mixture of two or more different fuels, as long as they are alike physically (i.e., liquid). Vehicles with flexible-fuel engines are not in widespread use anywhere to date.

Dedicated-fuel vehicles are designed to operate on a single alternative fuel. Typically cheaper and more efficient than the other two options, such vehicles (dedicated to LNG) are commonly used in taxis in Japan, Korea, and Thailand.

The Fuels

While there is still much active debate about which fuel or combination of fuels will eventually dominate the transportation scene, some are receiving more attention than others, in terms of both research budgets and demonstration projects. Alcohol fuels such as methanol and ethanol are among these fuels (although not always in a form created from renewable sources).

Alcohol fuels are converted from biomass (or other) feedstocks through one or more of the conversion technologies discussed in the previous chapter. Government and private research programs are currently working at finding more efficient, cost-effective methods of converting biomass to alcohol fuels for use in the transportation sector.

Methanol

Although methanol was originally a by-product of charcoal production, today it is primarily produced from natural gas. It can also be made from biomass and coal. When methanol is made from natural gas, the gas reacts with steam to produce synthesis gas, a mixture of hydrogen and carbon monoxide. This is then reacted catalytically at high temperatures and pressures to produce methanol. The process is similar if the methanol is produced by the gasification of biomass.

Ethanol

In the United States ethanol is mainly made from fermenting corn using either a dry-milling or a wet-milling process. In the dry-milling process, responsible for approximately one-third of the ethanol produced, the grain is milled without being first separated into its components. When the grain is mashed, the starch in the mash is converted to sugar and then to alcohol with yeast.

In the wet-milling process the corn is first separated into its major components (germ, which can be dried, separating out the oil, fiber, gluten, and starch). The starch can then be converted into ethanol. This process also yields salable by-products such as corn gluten feed and meal, which aid in the cost-competitiveness of the ethanol.

The only other country with a significant production of ethanol, Brazil, makes its fuel from sugarcane.

CNG

The fundamental difference between CNG and conventional motor fuels is its form: it is gaseous rather than liquid. Most gasoline-powered vehicles can be converted to a dual-fuel engine with CNG in a simple process that does not require the removal of any of the original equipment. Natural gas cylinders are mounted on the rear of the vehicle, and a fuel line runs the CNG from the cylinder to the engine through special mixer equipment. A switch installed in the dash selects either gasoline or CNG operation. Diesel vehicles can also be converted to a dual-fuel configuration with CNG.

Until recently, little research had been directed toward CNG-dedicated vehicles. There are two distinct approaches to the design of such vehicles: "lean-burn combustion" and "stoichiometric combustion" technologies. The former is derived from the standard design for a diesel engine, the latter, from that for a gasoline engine. While these designs do exist, converted dual-fuel vehicles using CNG are much more common than CNG-dedicated vehicles.

□ CURRENT STATUS

Fuel alcohol programs are appearing in more and more countries around the globe. Energy independence, low market prices for sugar and other food crops, and large agricultural surpluses are the primary reasons for these programs. The large majority of the countries developing fuel alcohol are in Africa and Latin America, with the exception of the United

States and a few other select countries. The United States is also an exception in that the main reason for its alcohol fuel program has to do with concerns about air quality.

Despite the increased use of alcohol fuels worldwide, however, they have yet to put a dent in the market for fossil fuels. Approximately 99 percent of all fuels consumed in road transport are still being produced from crude oil.

Methanol

In 1991 the U.S. methanol industry was producing approximately 3.8 million gallons of methanol per day. Of this, only about 38 percent was used as fuel for the transportation sector. Approximately 95 percent of fuel methanol is converted to MTBE rather than used in its pure form or as M85. Methanol is particularly popular in high-performance racing cars because of its octane-enhancing qualities.

In California there are more than 1,000 methanol-dedicated vehicles (cars, trucks, and buses) on the road in a program sponsored by the state with the participation of several auto manufacturers and oil companies. The California Energy Commission expects the number of light-duty vehicles using methanol to increase to approximately 5,600 flexible-fuel vehicles in California in 1992. New York City also has a number of buses that run exclusively on methanol.

The majority of the methanol produced in the United States at this time is from natural gas rather than from renewable biomass. While methanol can technically be made from biomass, more cost-effective and efficient methods are necessary before biomass can become the major source of methanol production.

Ethanol

Approximately 850 million gallons of ethanol are produced each year in the United States, primarily (95 percent) from the fermentation of corn. Much of this is used as a gasoline additive to produce a 10 percent ethanol/90 percent gasoline mixture called gasohol. About 30 percent of the nation's gasoline has some alcohol mixed with it. Most of the ethanol use in the United States is in the Midwest, where excess corn and grain crops are used as the feedstocks for this fuel.

In 1979 only twenty million gallons of fuel ethanol were being produced in the United States each year. This figure jumped to 375 million annually by 1983 and again to approximately 840 million annually in 1988.

More than sixty ethanol manufacturing facilities operate today in the United States, spread out across no fewer than twenty-two states. Farm vehicles have been converted to ethanol fuel, and demonstration programs are testing light-duty vehicles. The nation's first E85 (85 percent ethanol) fueling station opened in La Habra, California in 1990. The station is operated by the California Renewable Fuels Council as part of its research and demonstration programs in California.

Although most ethanol is currently generated from corn, researchers are concentrating on producing this alcohol fuel from cellulosic biomass (certain energy crops, forest residues, agricultural residues, and MSW), which has the potential of being a much cheaper feedstock. The process of chemically converting cellulosic biomass is currently more difficult, however, and until the process can be simplified the price of ethanol will remain relatively high.

Ethanol Production in Brazil

Brazil produces by far the most ethanol worldwide. The Brazilian government program to make ethanol from sugarcane began in 1975 and has resulted in more than four million cars in that country running on ethanol to date. The form of ethanol most widely used in Brazil is a mixture of 95 percent ethanol and 5 percent water (sometimes with a small amount—up to 3 percent—of gasoline).

Use of ethanol is widespread in Brazil. Nearly 90 percent of new cars run on neat ethanol, while the remaining 10 percent operate on a 20 percent ethanol/80 percent gasoline mix. Yet the country is able to produce this much ethanol using just 1 percent of its total farmable land. This is largely due to the fact that sugarcane can be grown almost year-round in Brazil. The program does not run without government assistance, however. In 1988 government subsidies for the production of ethanol from sugarcane amounted to approximately $1.3 billion.

The tremendous success of Brazil's program has actually resulted in some problems. Currently, the country is experiencing ethanol shortages because the more than fifteen billion liters produced annually is not enough to meet consumer demand. The Brazilian government is trying to import ethanol to meet the strong demand.

Reformulated Gasoline

Reformulated gasoline is making its mark on the alternative fuels map. Its main advantage is that automobiles do not need to be modified to use it. Because of its effectiveness in reducing tailpipe emissions, reformulated gasoline has qualified under the new Clean Air Act to compete with other alternatives as an option for meeting lower emission standards over the years to come.

Although actual "construction" can vary by manufacturer, reformulated gasoline typically has had polluting components like butane, olefins, and aromatics removed and an octane-enhancer like methyl tertiary butyl ether (MTBE) added. MTBE can reduce carbon monoxide by 9 percent, hydrocarbons by 4 percent, and nitrogen oxides by 5 percent, and improves combustion efficiency. It is used widely in such states as California, Arizona, and Nevada.

ARCO sells its reformulated gasoline, EC-1 Regular (Emission control-1), aimed at vehicles that still use leaded gasoline and do not have catalytic converters, in southern California. While these vehicles made up only 15 percent of the car and truck population of the area when ARCO introduced EC-1, they contributed a full 30 percent of the vehicular air pollution. ARCO has since introduced a gasoline for high-performance cars, EC-Premium. The EPA estimates that customers using the new ARCO reformulated gasolines are reducing air pollution by about 150 tons each day in southern California.

CNG

Even though the United States is one of the world's largest producers and consumers of natural gas, very little (3 percent of annual production) is used in the transportation sector. Problems with air quality and the large reserves of natural gas in this country have caused an increased interest in CNG as an automotive fuel in recent years.

CNG is used in approximately 30,000 vehicles in the United States, including school buses, delivery trucks, and fleet vehicles. Worldwide, nearly a million vehicles in at least thirty-five countries operate on CNG. Some of the countries in which natural gas is more widely used include New Zealand, Italy, and the former Soviet Union.

There are more than 300 CNG filling stations operating in the United States today. While most of these serve private fleets, about one-third are open to the public. This fuel is particularly appropriate for vehicles that operate in a reasonably limited geographical region and that can return to a central location every night for refueling.

In April 1991 the California Air Resources Board certified a CNG-powered engine as the first alternative-fueled engine certified for use in California. The board is also sponsoring a test program to fuel school buses with CNG in that state.

Flexible-fuel vehicles (FFVs)

One of the problems with the widespread development of alternative fuels is the chicken-and-the-egg dilemma. Should manufacturers make alternative-fuel vehicles without guaranteed fuel supplies? Or should the fuel industry begin widespread manufacture and distribution of a fuel (and which one?) without a guaranteed market? In other words, who begins the changeover?

Proponents of flexible-fuel vehicles (sometimes also called variable-fuel vehicles, or VFVs) say that their vehicles solve this dilemma. These vehicles are designed to use a variety of fuels as long as they are in the same physical state (i.e., liquid). Although FFVs are not yet in widespread use, the major automobile manufacturers have all developed prototypes for demonstration programs over the past decade, mostly focusing on methanol. The California Energy Commission expects to have more than 5,600 FFVs on the roads of that state by the end of 1992.

An FFV can detect which fuel is being used (or which mixture) and adjust accordingly. Sensors analyze the fuel before it reaches the engine and adjust the fuel delivery system, timing, and injectors as necessary. Volkswagen has reportedly developed an FFV that can run on any carbon-based liquid fuel, from diesel to alcohol.

FFVs are not without their critics, however. Some say that mixing methanol and gasoline in the same tank actually creates more ozone than gasoline does on its own. These critics say that mixing large quantities of gasoline with methanol increases the vapor pressure of the fuel, causing highly reactive hydrocarbons to escape into the atmosphere. This debate has yet to be resolved.

☐ BENEFITS AND CONCERNS

One of the more complicated aspects of alternative automobile fuels is that there is no clear winner—no obvious replacement for gasoline. Each alternative fuel, whether in use today or still in the development stage, has its advantages and disadvantages. The accompanying lists are not exhaustive, but they do note a few of the arguments for and against each of the alternative sources presented here. A more detailed discussion follows.

Clearly, there are issues relating to each of these alternative fuels that need to be researched further. In addition to technological and infrastructural developments, there are unanswered environmental questions. This is evidenced by the continuing debate over the specific environmental effects of each fuel. A lack of understanding of the long-term environmental effects from alternative fuels is one of the key concerns still to be resolved.

Both methanol and ethanol have some similar advantages and disadvantages in comparison to gasoline. Their octane ratings are higher than gasoline—this fact, and the resultant higher performance, make methanol popular among race car drivers.

Replacing gasoline with either methanol or ethanol would have significant environmental impacts. Pollutants such as unburned hydrocarbons and other volatile organic compounds (VOCs) that create ozone would be drastically reduced. Studies have shown that VOC emissions can be reduced by 85 to 95 percent, and carbon monoxide emissions can be reduced by 30 to 90 percent in cars designed specifically for alcohol fuels.

The higher octane allows for better efficiency, which may allow for smaller, lighter engines and lighter suspension/body parts. This could

METHANOL

(pure, unless otherwise noted)

ADVANTAGES

- high octane rating: 105
- renewable resource (if made from biomass)
- lower hydrocarbon emissions than gasoline: 35 percent lower for M85; up to 90 percent lower for M100
- produces less carbon dioxide when burned (although total depends on method of production)
- 30 to 40 percent lower total airborne toxins than gasoline (but formaldehyde emissions could be four to eight times higher than gasoline)
- less flammable in the open air than gasoline
- significantly reduced carbon monoxide emissions

DISADVANTAGES

- lower energy density than gasoline; driver must refill more frequently
- if swallowed, can blind or kill
- corrosion problems
- cold-start difficulties
- expensive

ETHANOL

(pure, unless otherwise specified)

ADVANTAGES

- high octane rating: 105
- renewable resource
- produces less carbon dioxide when burned than gasoline, but total impact depends on distillation process and efficiency of growing crops
- lowers carbon monoxide emissions when used as a gasoline additive
- less flammable than gasoline
- significantly reduced carbon monoxide emissions

DISADVANTAGES

- lower energy density than gasoline; driver must refill more frequently
- expensive
- as a gasoline additive, may create smog
- corrosion problems
- cold-start difficulties

Compressed natural gas (CNG)

Advantages

- high octane rating: 120
- currently inexpensive
- 40 to 90 percent lower hydrocarbon emissions than gasoline
- 50 to 90 percent lower carbon monoxide emissions than gasoline
- 10 percent lower carbon dioxide emissions than gasoline
- improved cold starting
- global and U.S. supplies more plentiful than those of oil

Disadvantages

- although currently plentiful, a nonrenewable resource
- larger, heavier fuel tank needed
- driver must refill every 100 miles and refilling takes two to three times longer than refilling gasoline ("slow fill" stations can take several hours)
- limited availability of filling stations (currently)

---

reduce automobile costs, or at least balance out any increases from new design requirements, and enhance the mileage from a gallon of alcohol fuel.

When these fuels are derived from biomass, the net increase in carbon dioxide emitted into the atmosphere is generally considered to be neutral or even negative because the plants used to produce the alcohol fuel have reabsorbed the same or more carbon than is emitted from the automobile. There is much debate whether this net effect is still as beneficial when the carbon dioxide emitted by machinery during the harvesting of the biomass feedstocks is taken into account. No conclusive answer has been reached because of the differences in equipment, farming techniques, and numerous other factors that vary from location to location.

When these fuels are derived from domestic biomass, their production creates jobs in agriculture and related industries. Expanded production could also increase export markets of co- and by-products (such as corn gluten meal, from ethanol).

Disadvantages shared by methanol and ethanol include lower energy density than that of gasoline. With both alcohol fuels as they are currently produced, the driver has to fill up the tank considerably more often than the driver of a car using gasoline. In addition, difficulty with cold starts can occur with both fuels in their neat form, but the addition of a small percentage of gasoline alleviates this problem.

Another common criticism of alcohol fuels, particularly methanol, is that they are corrosive to some of the automobile engine parts. This can be overcome by slight modifications to the materials used in the engine. Teflon tubing can replace rubber hoses, which are subject to corrosion, and nickel or stainless steel can be substituted for other metals.

Methanol

One of the major concerns regarding the widespread adoption of methanol as an automotive fuel is that its use emits higher amounts of formaldehyde, a contributor to ozone formation and a suspected carcinogen, than does gasoline. Proponents of methanol disagree, saying that only one-third of the formaldehyde from vehicle emissions actually comes from the tailpipe, with the other two-thirds forming photochemically, once the emissions have escaped. Thus, the argument goes, pure-methanol vehicles will generate only one-tenth as much of the hydrocarbons that are photochemically converted to formaldehyde as do gasoline automobiles. This issue is still a matter of some debate among experts.

Other concerns involve the fuel's colorless flame and explosive nature in a closed space (the tank). Low levels of colorants can easily be added to help identify the flame. Likewise, baffles or flame arresters located at the opening of the tank can prevent accidental ignition of methanol vapor.

Producing methanol from biomass (or coal) costs about twice as much as producing it from natural gas. As a result, economic pressures currently encourage the use of a nonrenewable source over biomass. If we take into account the full production cycle, methanol from biomass emits less carbon dioxide than ethanol from biomass. This is because short rotation forestry (the feedstocks of methanol) requires less fertilizer and diesel input than do agricultural starch and sugar crops (the feedstocks of ethanol).

Ethanol

More widespread use of ethanol could have some positive safety implications. The fact that ethanol is water soluble, biodegradable, and evaporates relatively easily means that, in the case of an ethanol spill, consequences are likely to be much less severe than in the event of a petroleum spill.

Of course, using agricultural surplus, as has been the case in the production of ethanol in the United States to date, can have economic benefits to farmers and to the economy in general. In 1989 alone, approximately 360 million bushels of surplus grain were used to produce ethanol. One estimate holds that in that year, as a direct result of ethanol production, farm income rose $750 million, federal farm program costs decreased $600 million, and crude oil imports fell by forty-two million barrels.

One of ethanol's major drawbacks in comparison to methanol is its price. It costs roughly twice as much as methanol currently.

Both methanol and ethanol, being liquids, would fit into the already-established storage and distribution infrastructure with little adjustment. This cannot be said for all other fuel options, including CNG.

CNG

CNG has several advantages over gasoline. It emits at least 40 percent less hydrocarbons and 30 percent less carbon dioxide per mile than gasoline. It is also quite inexpensive, currently about $0.70 per gallon-equivalent. Maintenance costs can also be less than those for gasoline automobiles because CNG causes less corrosion and engine wear.

Its main disadvantage in relation to all the fuels discussed here is that, although natural gas is a plentiful fossil fuel, it is still nonrenewable. There are other concerns as well. The range limitation is currently a severe drawback, and a CNG vehicle is expected to cost nearly $1,000 more than a gasoline vehicle because of the heavy cylinder used to keep the fuel under pressure. The weight and bulk of the CNG cylinders also take away storage space and reduce performance and fuel economy.

☐ COSTS

The current cost difference between gasoline and most alternative fuels is a major obstacle to the widespread use of these fuels. While further research is expected to make conversion technologies more efficient and therefore more cost-competitive, it is unclear what time frame will be required in order to accomplish this goal. As long as gasoline prices remain very low, it is unlikely that alternative fuels will reach cost-competitiveness without any help, either in the form of subsidies or tax credits.

Methanol currently costs about $0.75 per gallon. This fuel does not receive federal or state tax credits. Research over the last decade has managed to reduce the cost of wood-derived ethanol from $4.00 to between $1.10 and $1.35 per gallon before tax credits. The federal government currently provides tax credits of $0.60 per gallon, which is further subsidized by some states up to a further $0.40 per gallon. It is only because of these tax credits that the cost of ethanol is competitive with today's gasoline prices.

When talking about the per-gallon costs of methanol and ethanol, one must remember an important point: an accurate cost-comparison with gasoline requires multiplying the gallon cost by the number of gallons necessary to go the same distance as gasoline. For example, because methanol's energy density is about half that of gasoline, one must compare the cost of two gallons of methanol with that of one gallon of gasoline. Ethanol contains about two-thirds the energy per gallon as gasoline.

Costs for a gallon-equivalent of CNG vary widely. Whereas some sources cite prices as low as $0.70 per gallon-equivalent, others say prices can range as high as $1.20 per gallon-equivalent.

The Vehicle Costs

The cost to manufacture vehicles that run on alternative fuels has been the subject of much debate. Many believe that when all changes have been taken into account, the costs for neat-alcohol automobiles will be very close to the cost of a gasoline automobile (FFVs are expected to cost slightly more).

The EPA estimates that, with the necessary adjustments, the savings and costs will balance out to zero. It believes that the increased cost necessary for minor fuel tank adjustments to compensate for cold-start problems will be balanced out by the smaller, lighter engines neat-fuel cars can have because of their increased efficiency.

The case is slightly different with dual-fuel vehicles that could use CNG and a liquid fuel. Existing automobiles can be converted to run on CNG at a cost of approximately $2,000 (up to $3,500 for heavy-duty trucks and buses). The cost of a CNG-dedicated automobile is expected to be slightly higher than that of a gasoline automobile.

□ THE FUTURE

There is no doubt that the future holds a place for alternative fuels. Interest in their use is spreading, as evidenced by demonstration programs and commitments to expansion, small though they may be, by states such as California. Continued government tax credits will give the fuel producers an incentive to manufacture the fuels. Finally, the steady deterioration of air quality in many cities around the world makes finding a solution a more urgent requirement every day. What remains to be seen is which fuel or fuels emerge as the fuels of choice and to what extent alternative sources will replace gasoline. Experts believe that eventually a combination of available alternative fuels will be the most likely scenario.

To achieve a widespread penetration of alternative fuels, several obstacles will have to be overcome. These have to do with economic, technological, and infrastructural issues. First, the current situation in which gasoline holds the price advantage will have to change if alternative fuels are to become more commonplace. More efficient biomass conversion techniques will help make biofuels more cost-competitive. But it is also likely that until the price of oil rises, achieving cost-competitiveness will be extremely difficult.

Coordination is required between vehicle manufacturers, fuel producers, and the government. An appropriate infrastructure for the production and delivery of the fuels will be necessary, as will be the coordination of selections of fuels and the automobile adjustments necessary to run those fuels.

Finally, land availability and crop selection must be addressed if biomass is to be used on a significantly larger scale to produce transportation fuels. The availability in itself is not a problem, but the land use must be organized. It is expected that long-term production of biofuels in substantial quantities will require some changes in the crops used. For example, current grain surpluses will not provide sufficient feedstocks if fuel quantities grow substantially. It is expected that producers will switch to short-rotation woody plants and herbaceous grasses, the only feedstocks considered capable of sustaining biofuels production in long-term, substantial quantities. Likewise, the increased use of MSW as a feedstock for renewable fuels is likely.

Despite these hurdles, observers are optimistic about the role of alternative fuels in the future. The U.S. Department of Energy believes that by the year 2000 biofuels from nonfood crops and MSW could potentially cut U.S. oil imports by 15 to 20 percent. Ethanol industry members believe that the capacity for producing that fuel alone will double by 1995 and even triple by 2000.

7

ENERGY EFFICIENCY AND OUR ENERGY FUTURE

While energy efficiency is not the focus of this book, it has been mentioned often and deserves specific attention here because of its major importance to an all-encompassing, responsible energy strategy. It is important to emphasize that energy efficiency plays an important role in any responsible future energy policy.

Energy efficiency means getting the same work out of something for less energy. For example, efficient fluorescent light bulbs produce the same light but last much longer and use less electricity than regular light bulbs. Efficient automobiles go the same number of miles (or more) on less gasoline. These are just two examples. There are hundreds of technologies relating to energy efficiency that are applicable to consumers as well as to industry and to utilities.

It is a common fear that energy efficiency would mean "going without" things, or lowering our standard of living in the United States. But this nation has, in fact, increased its efficient use of energy dramatically over the past two decades. In 1989, for example, the country used only 7 percent more energy than it did in 1973. Yet its GNP has increased since 1973 by 46 percent. This is important for two reasons: it shows that Americans can, indeed, practice energy efficiency, and it shows that the country's growth need not be slowed by practicing energy efficiency.

The fact that historically the United States has done so well does not mean that it does not have the capability of much more efficiency; there is still a lot of room for improvement. For example, available technologies could more than double the efficiency of automobiles, appliances, lighting, space heating, and industrial processes.

Energy efficiency can be practiced in all aspects of our lives. Buildings can be made significantly more energy-efficient by installing insulation, and by placing windows in locations that can provide the best cooling in summer and the least heat escape in winter. The appliances we use in our homes—air conditioners, refrigerators, and clothes dryers, for example—can be made more efficient also. In fact, many manufacturers of consumer applicances are beginning to produce energy-efficient models of their products. Installing these in one's home can mean real energy— and cost—savings. And just as household appliances can be made more efficient, so can motors and other machinery used in industry. Cogeneration, or using heat wasted in the generation of energy to generate electricity, is one method that is becoming increasing popular.

Energy efficiency is important for many reasons. On a national level, efficiency makes the United States more competitive in international markets. If this country spent less energy to make its products (therefore dropping their prices), it would compete better with products from nations that practice better efficiency. In 1985, for example, Japan used 52.4 percent less energy per unit of GNP than the United States did, West Germany used 49 percent less, and Britain used 42.5 percent less.

Energy efficiency also benefits local economies, by providing employment. Technologies and services related to energy efficiency create more jobs than do the industries that generate energy. Finally, the benefit to the environment is clear, as has been shown. It is apparent that the environmental problems caused by current energy policies worldwide are of global proportions. What one country does affects another, and vice versa. We live today in an international community in which no country can ignore its neighbors, particularly in issues regarding energy and the environment.

Despite governmental policies or other potential barriers to development, renewable energy technologies *are* making inroads into the traditional energy infrastructure of this country and other nations around the globe. It has been shown that renewables like solar and wind power, hydropower, and biomass currently provide nearly 10 percent of the energy required by the United States, and that by conservative estimates these alternative energy sources—if used—could provide up to 75 percent of this energy in the next two or three decades. Experts believe this percentage could be much higher.

So, what can be done to encourage renewable energy development? Possibilities are almost endless. The government, industry, and individual citizens all have important roles to play in the development of a safe, viable energy future for this country—and parallel measures must be initiated around the globe. Only far-reaching measures affecting the whole range of our energy usage and production infrastructure will work.

We have seen that devastating environmental changes to our atmosphere are already a reality, and are worsening daily. Global warming, pollution, and changing climates are all real dangers that must be dealt with immediately. Fortunately, we have also seen that the means to deal with them are within our reach. Alternative energy technologies are available today and offer a real solution to many of our current environmental problems (not to mention political, economic, and social ones). The various chapters in this book have shown the current status of these renewable technologies and the new developments that are just around the corner.

They need help to develop. Current government policies are not implementing changes to encourage their development nearly to the extent necessary for a sound future. Business and industry are not investing in renewable technologies, and consumers are not purchasing renewable energy technology and energy-efficient products as much as they could. This is where we can all make a difference.

The measures our government can take are wide-ranging. An important step is to substantially increase the budget for R&D into renewable energy technologies. We have seen the (vastly) inequitable distribution of research funding from the U.S. Department of Energy, leaning heavily toward nuclear and fossil fuel research while virtually ignoring renewable technologies. This must be changed.

Not only do we need more funds directed toward renewable energy technologies, but funds should be directed at useful types of research. Rather than just funding basic research, it is imperative to develop projects that can help make renewable energy more attractive to industry. Helping to commercialize renewable technologies through joint ventures with industry and gearing research to practical applications are also important.

Once practical research programs have been established, these technologies still need help to move out of the laboratory and into the marketplace. Methods to help encourage market-readiness include constructing commercial-scale plants and manufacturing processes for newer technologies, developing and improving techniques for energy storage, and improving technical reliability. Close working relationships between government-sponsored research facilities and industry are necessary if such practical developments are to flourish.

Government policy can also take an important step in developing the viability of renewable technologies in the marketplace by not playing favorites with more conventional industries. Halting subsidies to the fossil fuel and nuclear industries (which put an unrealistically low price on their products), making tax breaks equitable, and looking at the full-cycle costs (including societal and economic costs) of energy sources when planning new capacity are all important ways of giving the newer industries a fair chance.

We have seen in earlier chapters that numerous hidden costs are involved in the generation of energy from fossil fuels or nuclear plants and that these are currently not included in price factoring. Some of the hidden costs of energy, produced largely from the environmental or political by-products of traditional energy sources, include agricultural losses, health costs, military expenditure, cleanup and storage of radio-active waste, and employment issues.

A very simple way in which the U.S. government can make a tremendous impact in the development of renewable energy technologies is by using them itself. It can, and should, lead by example. The sheer size of its annual budget means that the impact from a policy of purchasing renewable technology would be tremendous.

For example, government automobiles could all run on alternative fuels, all government buildings could use fluorescent light bulbs, solar water and space heating, and energy efficiency measures could readily be adopted throughout the government infrastructure. The impact of such policies would be overwhelming. In addition to fostering goodwill for renewable technology, the massive purchases would spur on the various industries, helping them to grow and develop, which would then lessen their need for government-sponsored support over time.

Setting standards that encourage, or require, renewable energy usage and energy efficiency are also important strategies. For example, establishing building standards that require greater insulation, improving mileage standards for automobiles, requiring production of more automobiles that run on alternative fuels—these are all steps the government can take. Greenpeace Action points out that achieving efficiency of up to sixty miles per gallon is both technically and economically feasible today, the result of which would be billions of dollars saved by the consumer at the gas pump and the avoidance of twenty-two billion barrels of oil over the next thirty years. The organization states that this saved oil is more than could be extracted offshore from the Pacific, Atlantic, and Alaskan coasts and in the Arctic National Wildlife Refuge combined.

The U.S. government has a responsibility to encourage the development of renewable energy technology in developing countries around the world. The result could be energy independence, decreased debt, and a healthier future for the citizens of these countries. The international community would also certainly benefit from no longer having to burn fossil fuels and rely on nuclear plants.

But while the U.S. government has a leadership role to play both in the implementation of sensible policies and by the practical application of renewable technologies, it cannot bear the burden alone. U.S. businesses and industries must take part also: they can encourage these energy sources by purchasing the technology and using it. Just as government buildings can be built with solar technology and methods that maximize energy efficiency, so can those of the corporate and industrial sectors.

The parallels between the government's ability to help and that of business and industry are strong. Corporate cars could run on alternative fuels, or at the very least, have standards of much higher fuel efficiency. Installing water-saving devices and energy-efficient light bulbs, raising the temperature of air conditioners, and lowering that for heating—all these are very important measures that could be initiated in business and industry across the nation. While these steps might seem minor, the energy savings would be tremendous: it has been estimated that the energy efficiency of buildings could be doubled by 2010, cutting in half carbon emissions and saving more than $100 billion annually.

For corporate and industrial America to adopt renewable energy technologies, it may well take a complete reversal of the philosophy that equates using less energy with restricting growth.

However, we have seen that this simply is not true. While the GNP in the United States has increased by approximately 46 percent since 1973, Americans use less than 10 percent more energy now than in 1973. So business and industry need to accept that profits do not have to fall in tandem with energy consumption.

Another way these sectors of society can help develop renewable energy technologies is by investing in them. As more investors can be found for these "newer" technologies, they will be able to obtain the same financing terms available to facilities using fossil fuel and nuclear energy, and hence will be able to compete better with these other energy sources.

Such investment in renewable energy technology will also help keep the technology in the United States, where Americans can benefit from its use, a number of citizens can be employed in the field, and consistent technological advances can enable the United States to compete better in the international market. (As noted earlier, a lack of investment by American companies has sent many developers overseas in search of companies to take their products.)

Finally, individuals have a very important role to play in the future development of renewable energy sources. People have much more power to influence the things around them than they perhaps realize sometimes, and that power can be put to excellent use by encouraging our elected officials to enact responsible environmental legislation, by purchasing appropriate renewable technology whenever possible, and by living our lives in a way consistent with a concern for the environment.

One of the most important ways Americans can influence the future is by voting. The power to vote politicians in or out of office is perhaps the best weapon in the fight against current energy policy—or lack thereof—in this country. Voters can let everyone in Washington and in their individual states know how they feel from the voting booth.

Study how representatives vote on environmental measures. Don't vote for people who—whether it be in the presidential race, for a Senate seat, or for the local city council—show no concern for the environment.

Vote for those who support renewable energy technologies and other environmental measures. Policies of the United States are not likely to change if individuals are elected who answer only to big corporations and traditional energy lobbies rather than think about the big picture—the future of the planet.

Election time isn't the only time to let elected officials know how citizens feel about environmental issues. Write to them about issues of concern. Banning oil exploration in the Arctic National Wildlife Refuge or off the Pacific coast, offering equitable financial incentives for renewable energy technologies, improving mileage efficiency in automobiles—these are just some of the issues every American can influence. Let elected officials know that if they don't support such measures, they will lose votes.

Write them detailed letters explaining what is needed. Demand that elected officials place a high priority on a safe, sensible energy policy that develops renewable energy technology and immediately lessens dependence on fossil fuels and nuclear energy. This is one way to ensure that a representative knows exactly what you want. And letters from voters count—most politicians will tell you that they pay attention to what their constituents say.

Not only do we have a lot of work to do as voters, we also have power as consumers. We can help develop renewable energy by using it whenever possible. Clearly, not all renewable energy technologies are applicable to individual uses, but many are, as are many energy efficiency measures. This book has given numerous examples of renewable energy technologies, some of which are practical for an individual, some not. Pick out the ones you can use and put them to work for you. If, on a larger-scale project, you can have some influence, then use that, too.

Although we have a lot of power as consumers, we often do not use this power wisely, simply because we do not think things through, or because we are trained to think of the short-term consequences of a purchase (i.e., initial price only) rather than the long-term ones. For example, when we purchase a refrigerator or an air conditioner, how many of us look at energy efficiency as a deciding factor in the purchase? Just as business and industry are used to looking at up-front costs and ignoring long-term savings, we as individual consumers tend to do the same.

Just as our votes show elected officials what we want, money talks, too. Our purchases show manufacturers, industry, and ultimately those same politicians that what we feel is important. This purchasing power must be used carefully and intelligently. We can write to manufacturers and tell them what we want. For example, we can write to American automobile manufacturers and tell them that we won't buy one of their automobiles until they reach the standards for mileage efficiency that we know they can attain.

Not only are our purchases important in sending signals to industry and government, they obviously have very practical consequences, too. By purchasing renewable energy technology, we can help establish these industries in the United States. The more customers these technologies can find within U.S. borders, the less likely it is that the United States will continue to export 65 percent of its renewable energy technology to other countries.

Whether we are looking at household appliances, or installing solar energy technology in our home, the issue of long-term saving is key. Quite often the environmentally sound decision is not the one that costs the least on the day of purchase. But these energy-efficient and renewable energy technologies will work out cheaper in the long run, as has been shown many times throughout this book. We need to train ourselves to take into consideration long-term savings when we make such purchases.

Solar energy technologies are perhaps the most applicable to individual homeowners and renters. Such solar applications as radiant barriers, solar hot-water and space heaters, and photovoltaic lighting can be installed in homes and will make a big difference in energy consumption. Geothermal heat pumps are another renewable energy technology that can be installed in individual residences and that results in reduced energy bills.

Using efficient appliances and taking other simple measures that have been discussed—using fluorescent bulbs, blocking drafts, planting trees, and installing insulation—can also cut energy consumption drastically.

In addition to purchases for our existing homes, many of us will, at some point in our lives, build (or have built) a house to our own specifications. This is an ideal opportunity to install numerous renewable energy devices and to take measures promoting energy efficiency. As was discussed in the solar energy chapter in particular, some devices are best installed during the construction of a house, so by thinking "renewable energy" at the outset, we have the opportunity of making our homes as environmentally sound as possible.

In addition to focusing specifically on our own homes, we can get involved locally to encourage the use of renewable energy technologies. The phrase "think globally, act locally" is used frequently, and it represents a very important philosophy. The things individuals do at the local level are multiplied across the country, so that what may seem a small act actually becomes part of a nationwide movement which can have an enormous effect on us all. Voting for local politicians is obviously an important first step. But there are many others to take, too. Participate in local environmental groups, and local chapters of national groups. These groups typically focus on issues specific to your area like cleaning up local beaches, protecting local waters from offshore drilling, or campaigning to get local utilities to switch to renewable energy sources.

Just as business and industry need to take a look at their environmental outlook and make a change in philosophy, many individuals could make a great contribution by doing the same. We would all profit from an overall philosophy of living in balance with our environment rather than carelessly destroying it. This involves not only helping the development of renewable energy technologies, but getting involved in the whole spectrum of activities that can make an important difference in our environment. Many of the suggestions offered here may sound easy— even silly because they are so obvious. But how many of us really perform these activities on a regular basis?

Recycling is increasing in popularity across this country. Many communities have now established curbside recycling programs wherein residents can put out their recyclable materials on the same day as their regular trash. Other recycling programs include drop-off sites, where you can take your recyclable materials, and pay-back centers, where you can be paid for some materials, typically aluminum and sometimes newsprint.

Recycling has many benefits. It saves precious natural resources (recycling plastic saves fossil fuels, but of course using plastics as little as possible in the first place saves even more!), landfill space, and energy. The energy savings can be dramatic: for example, making an aluminum can from recycled aluminum uses 95 percent less energy than making it from raw materials. Recycling glass, paper, and other metals saves energy, too.

We can dramatically cut down on the amount of energy we use simply by changing some of our habits:

- drying clothes on a line outside in warm weather

- when driving, combining errands on a single expedition rather than making five or six little trips by car every day (or better yet, walking or riding a bicycle to local errands)

- adjusting the thermostat two or three degrees higher on the air conditioner or lower on the heater

- sharing rides to school or work

- installing water-saving devices in toilets and shower heads.

These are all simple measures we can take if we think ahead and organize ourselves or simply make a conscious effort to include them in our routines. A massive effort by individuals across the country to make some of these changes would have an enormous effect on our energy consumption.

What does the future hold for our environment? The past decades have shown an increased interest in alternative energy sources and technologies and more environmental awareness in general among individuals across the globe—certainly positive signs in and of themselves. And as a result of increased knowledge, citizens tend to put pressure on governments, politicians, business, and industry to begin making necessary changes. Greater acceptance of the cost benefits of adopting policies beneficial to the environment will certainly help, but these ideas are slow to be recognized.

Unfortunately, policymakers are still not making the necessary commitment to an environmentally sound future. The consensus among scientists is that the problems of greenhouse gases and global warming, of pollution and dwindling nonrenewable energy supplies, are extremely serious. If we continue in a "business as usual" fashion, the consequences will be dire. Waiting until the problem gets any worse is not the answer.

Polluting fossil fuels and dangerous nuclear power plants must be replaced by the wide-ranging technologies available from renewable energy sources. The U.S. government must fund research into these technologies, and bring to market on a widespread basis those that are ready and functioning; it must use alternative energy technology within its own infrastructure.

This book has shown the full range of possibilities offered by renewable energy sources, and the variety of advantages they offer in addition to the environmental benefits. Economic, political, and social benefits will all be had by making the change to renewable energy.

Appendix: Sources of Information

1. SOLAR ENERGY

AMERICAN SOLAR ENERGY SOCIETY (ASES)
2400 Central Avenue, Suite B-1
Boulder, CO 80301
303/443-3130

ELECTRIC POWER RESEARCH INSTITUTE (EPRI)
P.O. Box 10412
Palo Alto, CA 94303
415/855-2000

FLORIDA SOLAR ENERGY CENTER
300 State Road 401
Cape Canaveral, FL 32920
407/783-0300

INTERSTATE SOLAR COORDINATION COUNCIL
900 American Center Building
St. Paul, MN 55101
612/296-4737

LUZ INTERNATIONAL
924 Westwood Boulevard, Suite 1000
Los Angeles, CA 90024
213/208-7444

NATIONAL RENEWABLE ENERGY LABORATORY
1617 Cole Boulevard
Golden, CO 80401
303/231-1000

SOLAR ELECTRIC
116 4th Street
Santa Rosa, CA 95401
707/542-1990

SOLAR ENERGY INDUSTRIES ASSOCIATION
777 North Capitol, NE, Suite 805
Washington, DC 20002
202/408-0660

2. WIND ENERGY

AMERICAN WIND ENERGY ASSOCIATION
777 North Capitol, NE, Suite 805
Washington, DC 20002
202/408-8988

ELECTRIC POWER RESEARCH INSTITUTE
P.O. Box 10412
Palo Alto, CA 94303
415/855-2000

EMBASSY OF DENMARK
3200 White Haven Street, NW
Washington, DC 20008
202/234-4300

KERN COUNTY WIND ENERGY ASSOCIATION
P.O. Box 277
Tehachapi, CA 93581
805/822-7956

U.S. WINDPOWER
6952 Preston Avenue
Livermore, CA 94550
510/455-6012

WEST TEXAS STATE UNIVERSITY
Alternative Energy Institute
P.O. Box 248, WT Station
Canyon, TX 79016-0248
806/656-2295

3. HYDROPOWER

**CALIFORNIA STATE DEPARTMENT
OF WATER RESOURCES**
Public Information Department
P.O. Box 942836
Sacramento, CA 94236
916/547-1155

HYDRO WIRE
HCI Publications
410 Archibald
Kansas City, MO 64111
816/931-1311

NATIONAL HYDROPOWER ASSOCIATION
555 13th Street, NW
Washington, DC 20004
202/637-8115

NORTHWEST SMALL HYDRO ASSOCIATION
P.O. Box 3610
Salem, OR 97306
503/363-0121

OAK RIDGE NATIONAL LABORATORY
P.O. Box 2008
Oak Ridge, TN 37831-6036
615/574-7305

SCRIPPS INSTITUTION OF OCEANOGRAPHY
University of California, San Diego
9500 Gilman Drive
La Jolla, CA 92093
619/534-6480

4. GEOTHERMAL ENERGY

GEO-HEAT CENTER
Oregon Institute of Technology
3201 Campus Drive
Klamath Falls, OR 97601
503/882-3583

GEOTHERMAL RESOURCES COUNCIL
P.O. Box 1350
Davis, CA 95617
916/758-2360

GEOTHERMAL RESOURCES COUNCIL OF NEVADA
P.O. Box 5151
Reno, NV 89513
702/784-6151

MERIDIAN CORPORATION
4300 King Street
Alexandria, VA 22302-1508
703/998-3600

**NATIONAL OCEANIC AND ATMOSPHERIC
ADMINISTRATION (NOAA)**
Federal Building
Asheville, NC 28801
704/259-0682

NATURAL RESOURCES DEFENSE COUNCIL
40 West 20th Street
New York, NY 10011
212/727-2700

U.S. GEOLOGICAL SURVEY
Geological Inquiries
907 National Center
Reston, VA 22092
703/648-4383

5. BIOMASS ENERGY

BIOMASS ENERGY INSTITUTE, INC.
1329 Niakwa Road East
Winnepeg, MB
Canada R2J 3T4
204/257-3891

BONNEVILLE POWER ADMINISTRATION
P.O. Box 3621
Portland, OR 97208
503/230-3449

MERIDIAN CORPORATION
4300 King Street
Alexandria, VA 22302-1508
703/998-3600

NATIONAL WOOD ENERGY ASSOCIATION
777 Capital, NE, Suite 805
Washington, DC 20005
703/524-6104

UNIVERSITY OF FLORIDA
Center for Biomass Energy Systems
Building 803, Room 11
Gainsville, FL 32611-0342
904/392-1511

U.S. DEPARTMENT OF ENERGY
Office of Renewable Energy Technologies
1000 Independence Avenue
Washington, DC 20585
202/586-4679

WESTERN AREA POWER ADMINISTRATION
1627 Cole Boulevard
P.O. Box 3402
Golden, CO 80401
303/231-1615

6. RENEWABLE AUTOMOBILE FUELS

AMOCO CORPORATION
200 East Randolph Drive
Box 87703
Chicago, IL 60680
312/856-6111

CALIFORNIA ENERGY COMMISSION
Public Information Department (MS-29)
1516 Ninth Street
Sacramento, CA 95814
916/654-4989

FORD MOTOR CO.
World Headquarters
The American Road
Dearborn, MI 48121
313/322-3000

NATIONAL CENTER FOR ATMOSPHERIC RESEARCH
Public Information Department
P.O. Box 3000
Boulder, CO 80307-3000
303/497-8612

PACIFIC GAS AND ELECTRIC
215 Market Street, Room 1416
San Francisco, CA 94106
415/973-7000

RENEWABLE FUELS ASSOCIATION
201 Massachusetts Avenue, NE, Suite C4
Washington, DC 20002
800/542-FUEL

U.S. DEPARTMENT OF ENERGY
Biofuels Division
1000 Independence Avenue, SW
Washington, DC 20585
202/586-4679

U.S. ENVIRONMENTAL PROTECTION AGENCY
Alternative Fuels Program
401 M Street
Washington, DC 20460
202/382-2080

GENERAL

CALIFORNIA ENERGY COMMISSION
1516 Ninth Street
Sacramento, CA 95814
916/324-3298

CALIFORNIA PUBLIC UTILITIES COMMISSION
360 McAllister Street
San Francisco, CA 94102
415/557-3914

CONSERVATION AND RENEWABLE ENERGY INQUIRY AND REFERRAL SERVICE (CAREIRS)
P.O. Box 8900
Silver Spring, MD 20907
800/523-2929

COUNCIL FOR RENEWABLE ENERGY EDUCATION
33 Hawk Pine Road
Norwich, VT 05055
802/649-2112

EMBASSY OF JAPAN
2520 Massachusetts Ave, N.W.
Washington, DC 20008
202/939-6700

GREENPEACE
1436 U Street, NW
Washington, DC 20009
202/462-1177

INDEPENDENT ENERGY
620 Central Avenue North
Milaca, MN 56353-1788
612/983-6892

INDEPENDENT ENERGY PRODUCERS ASSOCIATION
1001 G Street, Suite 103
Sacramento, CA 95814
916/448-9499

PUBLIC CITIZEN
Critical Mass Energy Project
215 Pennsylvania Avenue, SE
Washington, DC 20003
202/546-4996

PURPA LINES
HCI Publications
410 Archibald
Kansas City, MO 64111
816/931-1311

ROCKY MOUNTAIN INSTITUTE
1739 Snow Mass Creek Road
Snow Mass, CO 81654-9199
303/927-3128

SAFE ENERGY COMMUNICATION COUNCIL (SECC)
1717 Massachusetts Avenue, NW
Washington, DC 20036
202/483-8491

SANDIA NATIONAL LABORATORIES
P.O. Box 5800
Albuquerque, NM 87185
505/844-2433

SWEDISH EMBASSY
600 New Hampshire Avenue, NW
Washington, DC 20037
202/944-5600

UNION OF CONCERNED SCIENTISTS
26 Church Street
Cambridge, MA 02238
617/547-5552

U.S. AGENCY FOR INTERNATIONAL DEVELOPMENT
Directorate for Energy and Natural Resources
Washington, DC 20523
703/235-2243

U.S. DEPARTMENT OF ENERGY
National Appropriate Technology
Assistance Service (NATAS)
P.O. Box 2525
Butte, MT 59702-2525
800/428-2525

U.S. DEPARTMENT OF ENERGY
Office of Renewable Energy Technologies
1000 Independence Avenue
Washington, DC 20585
202/586-4679

U.S. EXPORT COUNCIL FOR
RENEWABLE ENERGY (US/ECRE)
P.O. Box 10095
Arlington, VA 22210/9998
202/408-0665

U.S. PUBLIC INTEREST RESEARCH GROUP (PIRG)
215 Pennsylvania Avenue, SE
Washington, DC 20003
202/546-9707

WORLDWATCH INSTITUTE
1776 Massachusetts Avenue, NW
Washington, DC 20036
202/452-1999

Bibliography

INTRODUCTION

"Americans Want More Efficient Cars." ENfacts series. Washington, D.C.: Safe Energy Communication Council, 1990.

BECKER, JONATHAN, ED. "Investing in Solar Energy: Recommendations for the U.S. Department of Energy's Research and Development Budget for Renewable Energy Technologies FY 1992–1994." 2nd ed. Washington, D.C.: Public Citizen, March 1991. (Available from Public Citizen, 215 Pennsylvania Avenue, SE, Washington, DC 20003 [202] 546-4996. Price: $10.00)

BYRNE, JEANNE. "Mythbusters #5: Renewable Energy." Washington, D.C.: Safe Energy Communication Council, 1990.

"Energy." Washington, D.C.: Greenpeace Action, 1991.

"Energy Efficiency Today." ENfacts series. Washington, D.C.: Safe Energy Communication Council, 1990.

"Energy Funding: On the Wrong Track." ENfacts series. Washington, D.C.: Safe Energy Communication Council, 1990.

"The Greenhouse Effect." Washington, D.C.: Greenpeace, 1992.

IDAHO NATIONAL ENGINEERING LABORATORY, ET AL. *The Potential of Renewable Energy*. Interlaboratory white paper prepared for the Office of Policy, Planning and Analysis. Washington, D.C.: U.S. Department of Energy, 1990.

NICKLAS, MICHAEL. "Societal Costs of Energy." In *ASES 1989 Roundtable: Societal Costs of Energy*. Boulder, Colo.: American Solar Energy Society, 1989, pp. 2–3.

RADER, NANCY, AND KEN BOSSONG. "Renewable Energy Poised to Triple by Year 2000." Washington, D.C.: Public Citizen, 1991. (Available from Public Citizen, 215 Pennsylvania Avenue, SE, Washington, DC 20003 [202] 546-4996. Price: $1.75)

"Renewable Energy: It's Ready Now." ENfacts series. Washington, D.C.: Safe Energy Communication Council, 1990.

SOLAR ENERGY RESEARCH INSTITUTE (SERI). "CORECT 1990—Committee on Renewable Energy Commerce and Trade." Golden, Colo.: SERI, 1991.

———. "Energy for Today—Renewable Energy." Golden, Colo.: SERI, 1990.

U.S. EXPORT COUNCIL FOR RENEWABLE ENERGY (US/ECRE). "Renewable Energy for the World, 1990." Arlington, Va.: US/ECRE, 1990.

1. SOLAR ENERGY

ANDERSON, JOHN V., AND P. GUPTA BIMLESHWAR. "Solar Detoxification of Hazardous Waste." *Solar Today* November/December 1990, pp. 10–13.

BANKSTON, CHARLES A. "Concentrating Collector Systems," In *Assessment of Solar Energy Technologies.* Boulder, Colo.: American Solar Energy Society, 1989, pp. 21–24.

BELLEVILLE, LAUREEN. "Solar Power Goes the Extra Mile." *Laser Focus World* February 1991, p. 48.

BIGGER, JOHN E., AND EDWARD C. KERN, JR. "Early Applications of Photovoltaics in the Electric Utility Industry." Paper presented at the 21st IEEE Photovoltaics Specialists Conference, Kissimmee, Florida, May 21–25, 1990.

BIGGER, JOHN E., ET AL. "Cost-Effective Photovoltaic Applications for Electric Utilities." Paper presented at the 22nd IEEE Photovoltaic Specialists Conference, Las Vegas, Nevada, October 7–11, 1991.

BLUM, SHEILA. "Working Together for a Solar Future." Washington, D.C.: International Energy Agency, 1991.

BORSON, DANIEL, ET AL. "A Decade of Decline." Washington, D.C.: Public Citizen, 1989. (Available from Public Citizen, 215 Pennsylvania Avenue, SE, Washington, DC 20003 [202] 546-4996. Price: $7.50)

BZURA, JOHN J. "Residential Photovoltaics: The New England Experience Builds Confidence in PV." In *Photovoltaics: New Opportunities for Utilities.* Golden, Colo.: Solar Energy Research Institute, 1991.

"California Utilities Plan Solar Energy Experiment." *Wall Street Journal* August 30, 1991, p. A3.

DEMEO, EDGAR A. "Photovoltaics for Bulk Power Applications: Cost/Performance Targets and Technology Prospects." Paper presented at the 10th European PV Solar Energy Conference, Lisbon, Portugal, April 8–12, 1991.

DEMEO, EDGAR A., ET AL. "Economic Requirements for Photovoltaic Systems in Electric Utility Applications." Paper presented at the IEA/ENEL Conference on Photovoltaic Systems for Electric Utility Applications, Taormina, Italy, December 2–5, 1990.

———. "Solar Photovoltaic Power: A U.S. Electric Utility R & D Perspective." Paper presented at the 21st IEEE Photovoltaic Specialists Conference, Orlando, Florida, May 21–25, 1990.

ELECTRIC POWER RESEARCH INSTITUTE (EPRI). "Amorphous Silicon Thin Films: The Next Step in Solar Cells." Palo Alto, Calif.: EPRI, 1991.

———. "Bringing Solar Electricity to Earth." Palo Alto, Calif.: EPRI, 1990.

———. "Electricity from Sun and Wind." Palo Alto, Calif.: EPRI, 1991.

"Energy Options." *Business Week* June 18, 1990, p. 78.

FLAVIN, CHRISTOPHER, AND NICHOLAS LENSSEN. *Beyond the Petroleum Age: Designing a Solar Economy.* Washington, D.C.: Worldwatch Institute, 1990.

————. "Designing a Solar Economy: A Policy Agenda." *Solar Today* May/June 1991, pp. 18–20.

FLORIDA SOLAR ENERGY CENTER (FSEC). "Photovoltaic Applications—A Guide for Decision-Makers." Cape Canaveral, Fla.: FSEC, 1989.

————. "Photovoltaics: A Question and Answer Primer." Cape Canaveral, Fla.: FSEC, 1985.

————. "Radiant Barriers: A Question and Answer Primer." Cape Canaveral, Fla.: FSEC, 1987.

GIPE, PAUL. "A Silver Lining." *Independent Energy* May/June 1990, pp. 67–68.

HESTER, S. L., AND T. U. TOWNSEND. "The Photovoltaics for Utility Scale Applications (PVUSA) Project in the United States." *Solar Today* May/June 1991, pp. 23–24.

HOFFNER, JOHN E., AND DAVID C. PANICO. "Photovoltaic Utilities." *Solar Today* July/August 1990, pp. 14–16.

HUBER, PETER. "Who Will Buy the Electric Car?" *Forbes* February 19, 1991, p. 166.

HULSTROM, ROLAND L., ED. *Solar Resources.* Cambridge, Mass.: MIT Press, 1989.

INTERNATIONAL ENERGY AGENCY (IEA). "Working Together for a Solar Future." Washington, D.C.: IEA, 1991.

KONRAD, WALLY. "Solar Energy's New Place in the Sun." *Business Week* October 7, 1991, p. 154.

LOTKER, MICHAEL, AND DAVID KEARNEY. "Solar Thermal Electric Performance and Prospects, the View From Luz." *Solar Today* May/June 1991, pp. 10–13.

MCFADDEN, PAM, AND DENNIS A. ANDREJKO. "Passive Heating." In *Assessment of Solar Energy Technologies,* pp. 9–11. Boulder, Colo.: American Solar Energy Society, 1989.

MCINNES, COLIN. "On the Crest of a Sunbeam." *New Scientist* January 5, 1991, pp. 31–33.

MELODY, INGRID. "Solar Water Desalination." *Solar Today* November/December 1990, pp. 14–16.

MOORE, TAYLOR. "On-Site Utility Applications for Photovoltaics." *EPRI Journal* March 1991, pp. 27–37.

NATIONAL ASSOCIATION OF HOME BUILDERS (NAHB) NATIONAL RESEARCH CENTER. "Solar Electric Houses Today." Upper Marlboro, Md.: NAHB, 1988.

OGDEN, JOAN M., AND ROBERT H. WILLIAMS. *Solar Hydrogen: Moving Beyond Fossil Fuels.* Washington, D.C.: World Resources Institute, 1989.

"Rapid Recharge for Batteries in Nissan's Electric Car." *New Scientist* September 7, 1991, p. 31.

SARGENT, STEPHEN L. "Solar Ponds." In *Assessment of Solar Energy Technologies.* pp. 24–26. Boulder, Colo.: American Solar Energy Society, 1989.

SCHAEFER, JOHN C., AND EDGAR A. DeMEO. "An Update on U.S.

Experience with Photovoltaic Power Generation." *Proceedings of the American Power Conference* May 1990, pp. 272–79.

SHEINKOPF, KENNETH G. "Passive Cooling." In *Assessment of Solar Energy Technologies*. pp. 11–13. Boulder, Colo.: American Solar Energy Society, 1989.

SKLAR, SCOTT, AND KENNETH SHEINKOPF. *Consumer Guide to Solar Energy.* Chicago: Bonus Books, 1991.

SOLAR ENERGY INDUSTRIES ASSOCIATION (SEIA). "Solar Electric Applications and Directory of the U.S. Photovoltaic Industry." Washington, D.C.: SEIA, 1991.

——. "Solar Energy Uses in the Utility Sector." Washington, D.C.: SEIA, 1990.

——. "Solar Industry Green Plan: A Call for Action." Washington, D.C.: SEIA, 1991.

SOLAR ENERGY RESEARCH INSTITUTE (SERI). "Focusing on the Future." Golden, Colo.: SERI, 1989.

——. "Photovoltaic Energy Program Overview FY 1990." Golden, Colo.: SERI, 1991.

——. "Photovoltaic Energy Program Summary, Vol. 1: Overview FY 1989." Golden, Colo.: SERI, 1990.

——. "Photovoltaics—Entering the 1990s." Golden, Colo.: SERI, 1989.

——. "Photovoltaics: From the Laboratory to the Marketplace." Golden, Colo.: SERI, 1991.

——. "Photovoltaics: Fundamentals." Golden, Colo.: SERI, 1991.

——. "Photovoltaics: New Opportunities for Utilities." Golden, Colo.: SERI, 1991.

——. "Photovoltaics Technical Information Guide." 2nd ed. Golden, Colo.: SERI, 1988.

——. "Solar Buildings Program Summary, Vol. 1: Overview FY 1989." Golden, Colo.: SERI, 1990.

——. "Solar Thermal Program Summary, Vol. 1: Overview FY 1989." Golden, Colo.: SERI, 1990.

"Solar Power: Energy for Today and Tomorrow." Cambridge, Mass.: Union of Concerned Scientists, 1990.

SWIFT, A., ET AL. "Commercialization of Solar Ponds." *Solar Energy* July/August 1990, pp. 17–18.

THOMAS, MICHAEL, ET AL. "Photovoltaic Systems for Government Agencies." Albuquerque, N. Mex.: Sandia National Laboratories, 1989.

TORO, TARYN. "Sunshine Brings Water to West Africa." *New Scientist* March 16, 1991, p. 27.

U.S. DEPARTMENT OF ENERGY (U.S. DOE). "Heating Your Home with an Active Solar Energy System." 3rd ed. Washington, D.C.: U.S. DOE, 1990.

——. "Passive and Active Solar Domestic Hot Water Systems." 3rd ed. Washington, D.C.: U.S. DOE, 1988.

————. "Passive Solar Heating." 3rd ed. Washington, D.C.: U.S. DOE, 1989.

WEINBERG, CARL J., AND ROBERT H. WILLIAMS. "Energy from the Sun." *Scientific American* September 1990, pp. 147–55.

WILSON, ALEX. "The Changing Solar Industry." *Independent Energy* March 1990, pp. 67–68.

————. "Consumer Products Lighting the Way." *Independent Energy* May/June 1990, pp. 64–66.

————. "Growing Markets." *Independent Energy* January 1990, pp. 41–42.

————. "Under New Management." *Independent Energy* February 1990, p. 52.

WILSON, HOWARD G., ET AL. "Lessons of Sunraycer." *Scientific American* March 1989, pp. 90–97.

WOODWARD, BRIAN. "Race to Find the Fastest Car under the Sun." *New Scientist* November 17, 1990, p. 29.

ZABUKOVER, J. "Photovoltaic Systems for the Rural Consumer." In *Photovoltaics: New Opportunities for Utilities*. Golden, Colo.: SERI, 1991, pp. 20–22.

2. WIND ENERGY

"Altamont Pass Windfarms." San Francisco: Pacific Gas and Electric and U.S. Windpower, 1988.

ALTERNATIVE ENERGY INSTITUTE, WEST TEXAS STATE UNIVERSITY. "Introduction to Wind Energy." 3rd ed. Canyon, Tex.: West Texas State University, 1990.

AMERICAN WIND ENERGY ASSOCIATION (AWEA). "California Energy Commission Staff Says Wind Good Buy." Washington, D.C.: AWEA, 1989.

————. "Wind Energy—a Resource for the 1990s and Beyond." Washington, D.C.: AWEA, 1991.

————. "Wind Energy for a Growing World (with a Directory of the U.S. Wind Industry)." Washington, D.C.: AWEA, 1990.

————. "Wind Energy in the 80s—a Decade of Development." Washington, D.C.: AWEA, 1990.

————. "Wind Energy One of State's Least Cost Sources for New Electricity Generation Says Energy Commission." Washington, D.C.: AWEA, 1990.

ASSOCIATION OF DANISH WINDMILL MANUFACTURERS/FDV. *Wind Power in the 90's—Pure Energy*. Herning, Denmark: Association of Danish Windmill Manufacturers, 1991.

BROWN, LINDA. "Wind Power: Today's Energy Option." *Solar Today* July/August 1990, pp. 10–13.

CONOVER, KAREN, AND DAN SELIGMAN. "Environmental Issues Associated with Wind Power Generation." Paper presented at the American Wind Energy Association "Wind Power 1990" Conference, Washington, D.C., September 1990.

"Danish Elkraft Moves Offshore." *Independent Energy* January 1990, p. 48.

DODGE, D. M., AND R. W. THRESHER. "Wind Energy." In *Assessment of Solar Energy Technologies*, pp. 31–34. Boulder, Colo.: American Solar Energy Society, 1989.

FLOOD, MIKE. "Danish Wind Farms Head Out to Sea." *New Scientist* October 20, 1990, p. 26.

GIPE, PAUL. "Breaking Out of California." *Independent Energy* September 1990, p. 62 + .

———. "Capacity Down—Outlook Up." *Independent Energy* February 1990, pp. 60–63.

———. Communication with author, April 23, 1992.

———. "New Attitudes toward Wind." *Independent Energy* March 1990, p. 62 + .

———. "Progress in California." *Independent Energy* January 1990, pp. 45–64.

———. "Utility Interest in Wind Grows." *Independent Energy* July/ August 1990, pp. 68–69.

———. "Wind Energy Comes of Age in California." Tehachapi: Paul Gipe and Assoc., July 1989.

———. "Wind Generation Up Dramatically." *Independent Energy* April 1990, p. 46.

———. "Windpower: Status Report, 1991." *Independent Energy* September 1991, pp. 60–64

KING, WILLIAM R., AND BERTRAND L. JOHNSON III. "Worldwide Wind/ Diesel Potential." *Independent Energy* September 1991, pp. 66–69.

LYNETTE, ROBERT. "Status and Potential of Wind Energy Technology." Paper presented at the American Wind Energy Association "Wind Power 1990" Conference, Washington, D.C., September 1990.

MILBORROW, D. J. "Energy from the Wind." *Contemporary Physics* vol. 31, no. 3, pp. 165–78

MILNE, ROGER. "Britain 'Squandering' the Best Wind in Europe." *New Scientist* September 29, 1990, p. 16.

———. "Windfall for Scotland's Renewable Power." *New Scientist* March 2, 1991, p. 27.

MOORE, TAYLOR. "Excellent Forecast for Wind." *EPRI Journal* June 1990, pp. 15–25.

"Noise." *Windpower Monthly* August 1990, pp. 12–19.

NORRIS, CARINA. "Turbines Turn Motorways into a Source of Power." *New Scientist* September 29, 1990, p. 33.

POORE, ROBERT Z., AND ROBERT LYNETTE. "Wind Energy Cost Reductions Potential Technological Contributions." Paper presented at the 10th American Society of Mechanical Engineers Wind Symposium, Houston, Texas, January 20–23, 1991.

SOLAR ENERGY RESEARCH INSTITUTE (SERI). "SERI's Unique Blades May Give New Things to the U.S. Wind Industry." Golden, Colo.: SERI, 1990.

————. "Wind Energy Program Summary, Vol. 1: Overview FY 1989." Golden, Colo.: SERI, 1990.

SERI, SOLAR TECHNICAL INFORMATION PROGRAM. "An Old Idea Takes New Shape for Electric Utilities." Palo Alto, Calif.: Electric Power Research Institute, 1990.

SERI, TECHNICAL INFORMATION PROGRAM. "Cost of Wind Energy." Palo Alto, Calif.: Electric Power Research Institute, 1991.

SWISHER, RANDALL. "Wind Energy Comes of Age." *Solar Today* May/June 1991, pp. 14–17.

"The Tehachapi Wind Industry." Tehachapi: Kern Wind Energy Association, November 19, 1990.

VOGEL, SHAWNA. "Wind Power." *Discover* May 1989, pp. 47–49.

WALD, MATTHEW L. "Putting Windmills Where It's Windy." *The New York Times* November 14, 1991, Bus. p. 1.

"Wind Energy Rising . . ." *Environment* vol. 32, no. 4, May 1990, p. 23.

3. HYDROPOWER

"Anaheim Firm Eyes Wave Power." *Santa Cruz Sentinel* July 15, 1991.

"Barrages to Harness the Power of the Open Sea." *New Scientist* December 3, 1988, p. 38.

CHAPPELL, JOHN R., ET AL. "DOE Hydropower Program Biennial Report, 1990–1991." Idaho: U.S. DOE Field Office, 1991.

FAY, JAMES. "Harnessing the Tides." *Technology Review* July 1983, pp. 50+.

GALVIN, CYRIL. "Prospects for Wave Power." *Coastal Engineer Notes* August 1990, pp. 1–2.

GREENBERG, DAVID A. "Modeling Tidal Power." *Scientific American* November 1987, pp. 128–31.

HUNT, RICHARD T. "The High Cost of Hydro Licensing." *Independent Energy* October 1990, p. 44+.

IDAHO DEPARTMENT OF WATER RESOURCES, BUREAU OF ENERGY RESOURCES. *The Micro Hydro Handbook.* Boise, Idaho: Idaho Department of Water Resources, 1983.

LAGASSA, GEORGE. "Complying with the FERC." *Independent Energy* September 1990, pp. 56–59.

————. "Hydroelectric Monitoring in the 1990s." *Independent Energy* May/June 1990, pp. 58–62.

————. "Losing Out at Relicensing." *Independent Energy* September 1990, pp. 55–58.

————. "Turbine Competition Sharpens." *Independent Energy* January 1990, pp. 24–62+.

LEE, KAI N. "The Columbia River Basin Experimental Sustainability." *Environment* July/August 1989, pp. 6–11+.

LOUPE, DIANE. "The Food Factor: Spin-off Industries Make Ocean Energy Profitable." *Sea Frontiers* March/April 1991, pp. 22–27.

MILNE, ROGER. "Testing the Ground for the Severn's Tidal Power." *New Scientist* September 24, 1987, p. 35.

———. "Tidal Power Ruffles Feathers." *New Scientist* May 6, 1988, pp. 38–39.

MIYAZAKI, TAKEAKI. "Wave Power Generator 'Kaimei'." *Oceanus* Spring 1987, pp. 43–44.

NEWMAN, J. N. "Power from the Waves." *Technology Review* July 1983, pp. 51+.

PEARCE, FRED. "A Damned Fine Mess." *New Scientist* May 4, 1991, pp. 36–39.

QUIDDINGTON, PETER. "Indians Cheer Halt to Canada's Giant Hydro Scheme." *New Scientist* May 25, 1991, p. 17.

RAILSBACK, S. F., ET AL. "Environmental Impacts of Increased Hydroelectric Development at Existing Dams." Oak Ridge, Tenn.: Oak Ridge National Laboratory, 1991.

ROSS, DAVID. *Energy from the Waves*, 2nd ed. Oxford and New York: Pergamon Press, 1981.

———. "Europe Changes Tack on Energy from Waves." *New Scientist* February 9, 1991, p. 31.

———. "Europe Misled over Wave Energy." *New Scientist* November 10, 1990, p. 26.

———. "World's First Commercial Wavepower Stations Sold." *Alternative Sources of Energy* May/June 1987, pp. 55–56.

RUSTEBAKKE, HOMER M., ED. *Electric Utility Systems and Practices*. New York: Wiley,, 1983.

SALOMON, ROBERT E. "Rocking Buoy Wave Energy Converter." *Ocean Engineering* vol. 16, no. 3, pp. 319–24.

SOLAR ENERGY RESEARCH INSTITUTE (SERI). "Ocean Energy Program Summary, Vol. 1: Overview FY 1989." Golden, Colo.: SERI, 1990.

STERLING, RICK, P.E. Letter from Sterling (resource development and conservation section manager, State of Idaho Department of Water Resources) to author, December 2, 1991.

U.S. DEPARTMENT OF ENERGY (U.S. DOE). "DOE Hydropower Program Biennial Report 1990–1991." Idaho: U.S. DOE Field Office, 1991.

———. "Small-Scale Hydropower Systems." Washington, D.C.: U.S. DOE, 1988.

Utilization of Ocean Waves—Wave to Energy Conversion. Proceedings of an international symposium sponsored by the Waterway, Port, Coastal and Ocean Division of the American Society of Civil Engineers and the National Science Foundation, Scripps Institute of Oceanography, La Jolla, California, June 16–17, 1986. New York: American Society of Civil Engineers, 1987.

4. GEOTHERMAL ENERGY

ANDERSON, DAVID N., AND JOHN W. LUND. "Geothermal Resources." In *Encyclopedia of Physical Science and Technology*, vol. 6, pp. 1–31. New York: Academic Press, Inc., 1987.

ANDERSON, IAN. "Blowout Blights Future of Hawaii's Geothermal Power." *New Scientist* July 20, 1991, p. 17.

AXELSSON, GUDNI. "Reservoir Engineering Studies of Small Low-Temperature Hydrothermal Systems in Iceland." *GHC Bulletin* April 1991, pp. 16–19. (Summary of a paper presented at the 16th Workshop on Geothermal Reservoir Engineering, Stanford University, Stanford, California, January 23–25, 1991.)

BARKER, B. J., ET AL. "Geysers Reservoir Performance." *GHC Bulletin* August 1991, pp. 1–14.

"A Boost for Geothermal Energy." *Environment* vol. 30, no. 2 March 1988, pp. 23–24.

BOWEN, ROBERT. *Geothermal Resources,* 2nd ed. London and New York: Elsevier Applied Science, 1989.

"Conference on Energy and the Environment Takes Look at Worldwide Geothermal Development." *Geothermal Progress Monitor* December 1990, pp. 51–52.

"Developer Drills at Crater Lake Border." *National Parks* January/February 1990, pp. 9–10.

EARTH SCIENCE LABORATORY, UNIVERSITY OF UTAH RESEARCH INSTITUTE (UURI). "Geothermal Energy." Salt Lake City: UURI, 1991.

ENERGY INFORMATION ADMINISTRATION, U.S. DOE. "Geothermal Energy in the Western United States and Hawaii: Resources and Projected Electricity Generation Supplies." Washington, D.C.: U.S. DOE, 1991.

"Environmental Merits of Geothermal Energy Noted at "Conference on Energy and the Environment in the 21st Century." *Geothermal Progress Monitor* December 1990, pp. 23–24.

"Fahrenheit 932." *Discover* August 1988, p. 12.

"First Utility Geothermal Power Planned for the Pacific Northwest." *Geothermal Progress Monitor* December 1990, pp. 26–27.

GEOTHERMAL EDUCATION OFFICE. "About Geothermal Energy." South Deerfield, Mass.: Channing L. Bete, 1990.

"Geothermal Heat Pumps—Emerging Giant?" *Geothermal Progress Monitor* December 1990, pp. 28–29.

GIPE, PAUL. "Losing Steam at The Geysers." *Independent Energy* February 1990, pp. 56–57.

HAMMONS, T. J., ET AL. "Geothermal Electric Power Generation in Iceland for the Proposed Iceland/United Kingdom HVDC Power Link." *IEEE Transactions on Energy Conversion* vol. 6, no. 2, June 1991, pp. 289–96.

HANNAH, LEE. "Rain-Forests and Geothermal Energy in Hawaii: Environmental Concerns Expose Flawed State Planning-Process." *Environmental Conservation* vol. 17, no. 3, Autumn 1990, pp. 239–44.

"The Hot Seat—Renewable Questions and Answers." *The Steam Press* Fall 1990, p. 2.

LEMONICK, MICHAEL D. "Hot Tempers in Hawaii." *Time* August 13, 1990, p. 68.

LIENAU, PAUL J. "Direct Heat." Prepared for GRC Introduction to Geothermal Resources, March 1990.

———. "Geothermal Aquaculture Development." *Geo-Heat Center Bulletin* April 1991, pp. 5–7.

———. Letter to author, October 28, 1991.

LUND, JOHN W. "Geothermal Spas in Czechoslovakia." *GHC Bulletin* Winter 1990, pp. 20–24.

LUND, JOHN W., ET AL. "The Current Status of Geothermal Direct Use Development in the United States Update: 1985–1990." Klamath Falls, Oreg.: Geo-Heat Center, 1990.

LUNIS, BEN. "Geopressured-Geothermal Direct Use Potentials Are Significant." *GHC Quarterly Bulletin* Winter 1990, pp. 1–7.

MARDON, MARK. "Steamed Up over Rainforests." *Sierra* May/June 1990, pp. 80–82.

MILNE, ROGER. "Britain Abandons Power from Hot Rocks." *New Scientist* February 16, 1991, p. 27.

MILSTEIN, MICHAEL. "Discoveries in the Deep." *National Parks* March/April 1990, pp. 29–33.

"PG&E to Shut Down Four Geothermal Plants." *Santa Cruz Sentinel* March 1991.

REED, MARSHALL J. "Geothermal Energy." *Geotimes* February 1990, pp. 24–25.

———. "Geothermal Energy." *Geotimes* February 1991, pp. 16–18.

SOLAR ENERGY RESEARCH INSTITUTE (SERI). "Geothermal Energy Program Summary, Vol. 1: Overview FY 1989." Golden, Colo.: SERI, 1990.

U.S. DEPARTMENT OF ENERGY (U.S. DOE). "Geothermal Energy." 2nd ed. Washington, D.C.: U.S. DOE, 1989.

5. BIOMASS ENERGY

BIOENERGY PROJECTS DIGEST/COMBUSTION, 1984–1989. Ottawa, Ontario: Efficiency and Alternative Energy Technology Branch, CANMET/Energy, Mines and Resources Canada, 1990.

BIOENERGY PROJECTS DIGEST/MATERIALS HANDLING, 1984–1989. Ottawa, Ontario: Efficiency and Alternative Energy Technology Branch, CANMET/Energy, Mines and Resources Canada, 1990.

BIOENERGY PROJECTS DIGEST/THERMOCHEMICAL CONVERSION, 1984–1989. Ottawa, Ontario: Efficiency and Alternative Energy Technology Branch, CANMET/Energy, Mines and Resources Canada, 1990.

"Biomass Energy: The Forgotten Fuel." *Biologue* May/June 1991, pp. 10–16.

"Biomass Oil—A Renewable Fuel." *Geotimes* May 1990, p. 6.

CARLESS, JENNIFER. *Taking Out the Trash: A No-Nonsense Guide to Recycling.* Washington, D.C.: Island Press, 1992.

COOK, JAMES H., ET AL. "Toward Sustainable Biomass Energy." *Biologue* September 1991, pp. 5–9.

COOKE, RICHARD. "A Cow Manure Fueled Power Plant." *Solar Today* November/December 1990, pp. 18–20.

DE GROOT, P. "Plant Power: Fuel for the Future." *New Scientist* December 16, 1989, pp. 30–33.

McCARTY, PARTICK, AND THAIR JORGENSON. "Fluidized Bed for Resource Recovery." *Independent Energy* October 1990, pp. 40–42.

MILES, THOMAS R., AND THOMAS R. MILES, JR. "Urban Wood: Fuel from Landscapers and Landfills." *Biologue* September 1991, pp. 10–12.

MILNE, ROGER. "Fuel Growers Call for Government Support." *New Scientist* March 23, 1991, p. 27.

RADER, NANCY, ET. AL. "The Power of the States: A Fifty-State Survey of Renewable Energy." Washington, D.C.: Public Citizen, 1990. (Available from Public Citizen, 215 Pennsylvania Avenue, SE, Washington, DC 20003 [202] 546–4996. Price: $20.00)

RINEBOLT, DAVID C. "Biomass Energy: A Maturing Industry." *Biologue* November, December 1989/January 1990, pp. 20–23.

————. Testimony (of the director of research, National Wood Energy Association) before the House Appropriations Committee, Energy and Water Development Subcommittee, Washington, D.C., April 3, 1990.

SOLAR ENERGY RESEARCH INSTITUTE (SERI). "Biofuels Program Summary, Vol. 1: Overview FY 1989." Golden, Colo.: SERI, 1990.

U.S. AGENCY FOR INTERNATIONAL DEVELOPMENT (U.S. AID) Office of Energy. "Power for the Grid from Sugarcane Residues." Washington, D.C.: U.S. AID, 1989.

U.S. BIOMASS INDUSTRIES COUNCIL (US/BIC). "The Biofuels Directory." Arlington, Va.: US/BIC, 1990.

U.S. DEPARTMENT OF ENERGY (U.S. DOE). "Biofuels as a Source of Energy." 1st ed. Washington, D.C.: U.S. DOE, 1987.

————. "Five Year Research Plan, 1988–1992. Biofuels: Renewable Fuels for the Future." Washington, D.C.: U.S. DOE, 1988.

WESTERN REGIONAL BIOMASS ENERGY PROGRAM. "Biomass Energy: Project Planning and Development." Golden, Colo.: Western Regional Biomass Energy Program, 1987.

————. "Biomass Energy: A Resource Assessment." Golden, Colo.: Western Regional Biomass Energy Program, 1987.

WINROCK INTERNATIONAL. "Energy from Rice Residues." Arlington, Va.: Winrock International, 1990.

————. "Industrial Energy and Electric Power from Wood Residues." Arlington, Va.: Winrock International, 1991.

6. RENEWABLE AUTOMOBILE FUELS

"Alternative Fuels." *Business Week* June 18, 1990, p. 50.

BLEVISS, DEBORAH L., AND PETER WALZER. "Energy for Motor Vehicles." *Scientific American* September 1990, pp. 103–9.

BURNETT, W. M., AND S. D. BAN. "Changing Prospects for Natural Gas in the United States." *Science* April 21, 1989, pp. 305–10.

CALIFORNIA ENERGY COMMISSION. "Clean, Alternative Fuels Programs." Sacramento: California Energy Commission, 1991.

———. "Methanol Vehicle Fact Sheet." Sacramento: California Energy Commission, 1991.

"The Car That Drinks Cocktails." *The Economist* September 28, 1991, pp. 105–6.

COLLINGE, ROBERT A., AND ANNE STEVENS. "Targeting Methanol or Other Alternative Fuels: How Intrusive Should Public Policy Be?" *Contemporary Policy Issues* vol. 3, January 1990, pp. 54–61.

DINNEEN, ROBERT. "Congress Acts to Increase the Production of Ethanol." *Biologue* March/April 1991, pp. 11–13.

———. "Ethanol: Clean Fuel for the '90s." *Biologue* September/October 1990, pp. 10–12.

DOSTROVSKY, ISRAEL. "Chemical Fuels from the Sun." *Scientific American* December 1991, 102–7.

"Fact Sheet: Natural Gas as a Transportation Fuel." Chicago, Ill.: Amoco Corporation, 1991.

FRAAS, ARTHUR, AND ALBERT McGARLAND. "Alternative Fuels for Pollution Control: An Empirical Evaluation of Benefits and Costs." *Contemporary Policy Issues* January 1990, pp. 62–74.

"The Fuels of the Future." *Consumer Reports* January 1990, pp. 11–15.

GOODMAN, BARBARA, AND GARY COOK. "Fueling the Future." *Solar Today* March/April 1990, pp. 18–20.

GRAY, CHARLES L., AND JEFFREY A. ALSON. "The Case for Methanol." *Scientific American* November 1989, pp. 108–14.

KUPFER, ANDREW. "The Methanol Car in Your Future." *Fortune* September 25, 1989, pp. 71+.

LALUCE, CECILIA. "Current Aspects of Fuel Ethanol Production in Brazil." *Critical Reviews in Biotechnology* vol. 2, no. 2, pp. 149–61.

LAREAU, THOMAS J. "The Economics of Alternative Fuel Use: Substituting Methanol for Gasoline." *Contemporary Policy Issues* vol. 8, October 1990, pp. 138–52.

LYND, LEE R., ET AL. "Fuel Ethanol from Cellulosic Biomass." *Science* March 15, 1991, pp. 1318–23.

MILLS, G. ALEX, AND E. EUGENE ECKLAND. "Alternative Fuels: Progress and Prospects." *Chemtech* October 1989, pp. 626–31.

"Natural Gas as a Transportation Fuel—Clean, Safe, and Economical." Chicago, Ill.: Amoco Corporation, 1991.

"Natural Gas Vehicles to Get Fuel Stations in California." *Wall Street Journal* June 19, 1991, p. A6.

NEILL, D., ET AL. "Renewable Transportation Alternatives." *Solar Today* July/August 1990, pp. 21–24.

"The New Clean Air Act: What It Means to You." *EPA Journal* vol. 17, no. 1, January/February 1991, pp. 12–17.

"1991 General Motors Public Interest Report." Detroit, Mich.: General Motors Corporation, 1991.

OKKEN, P. A. "A Case for Alternative Transport Fuels." *Energy Policy* May 1991, pp. 400–405.

"One for the Road—Will Alcohol-Fueled Cars Take Off or Backfire?" *Scientific American* December 1988, pp. 110–11.

REECE, NANCY S. "On the Road to an Alternative-Fueled Future, The Alternative Motor Fuels Act in Brief." *Solar Today* March/April 1991, pp. 10–12.

ROGNER, H.-H. "Natural Gas as the Fuel for the Future." *Annual Review of Energy* vol. 14, 1989, pp. 47–73.

RUSSELL, A. G., ET AL. "Ozone Control and Methanol Fuel Use." *Science* January 1990, pp. 201–4.

SATHAYE, JAYANT, ET AL. "Promoting Alternative Transportation Fuels: The Role of Government in New Zealand, Brazil, and Canada." *Energy* vol. 14, no. 10, pp. 575–84.

SOLAR ENERGY RESEARCH INSTITUTE (SERI). "Biofuels Program Summary, Vol. 1: Overview FY 1989." Golden, Colo.: SERI, 1990.

———. "Compressed and Liquefied Natural Gas—Just the Facts." Golden, Colo.: SERI, 1991.

———. "Conservation and Renewable Energy Technologies for Transportation." Golden, Colo.: SERI, 1990.

———. "Ethanol from Biomass—Just the Facts." Golden, Colo.: SERI, 1991.

———. "In Brief: The Alternative Motor Fuels Act." Golden, Colo.: SERI, 1991.

———. "Methanol Fuels—Just the Facts." Golden, Colo.: SERI, 1991.

SPERLING, D. *New Transportation Fuels: A Strategic Approach to Technological Change.* Berkeley: University of California Press, 1988.

———. "Toward Alternative Transportation Fuels." *Issues in Science and Technology* Fall 1990, pp. 30–33.

STRAWN, NONI. "Alcohol Fuels: Alternatives for Today and the Future." *Biologue* September/October 1990, pp. 13–17.

"U.S. CNG Fuel Marketing Push Accelerating." *Oil & Gas Journal* May 6, 1991, p. 44.

U.S. DEPARTMENT OF ENERGY (U.S. DOE). "Biofuels as a Source of Energy." Washington, D.C.: U.S. DOE, 1987.

U.S. ENVIRONMENTAL PROTECTION AGENCY (U.S. EPA), OFFICE OF MOBILE SOURCES SPECIAL REPORT. "Analysis of the Economic and Environmental Effects of Compressed Natural Gas as a Vehicle Fuel, Volume II, Heavy-Duty Vehicles." Washington, D.C.: EPA Office of Mobile Sources, 1990.

———. "Analysis of the Economic and Environmental Effects of Ethanol as an Automotive Fuel." Washington, D.C.: EPA Office of Mobile Sources, 1990.

———. "Analysis of the Economic and Environmental Effects of Methanol as an Automotive Fuel." Washington, D.C.: EPA Office of Mobile Sources, 1989.

"Which Gasoline for Your Car?" *Consumer Reports* January 1990, pp. 8–10.

WYMAN, CHARLES E., AND NORMAN D. HINMAN "Ethanol—Fundamentals of Production from Renewable Feedstocks and Use as a

Transportation Fuel." *Applied Biochemistry and Biotechnology* vol. 24/25, Spring 1990, pp. 735–53.

7. ENERGY EFFICIENCY AND OUR ENERGY FUTURE

ABELSON, PHILIP H. "National Energy Strategy." *Science* March 22, 1991, p. 1405.

ALLIANCE TO SAVE ENERGY, ET AL. *America's Energy Choices: Investing in a Strong Economy and a Clean Environment (Executive Summary)*. Cambridge, Mass.: Union of Concerned Scientists, 1991.

AMERICAN WIND ENERGY ASSOCIATION (AWEA). "National Energy Strategy Recommendations—American Wind Energy Association." Washington, D.C.: AWEA, 1990.

"ASES Recommendations for a National Strategy." *Solar Today* November/December 1990, p. 9.

BECKER, JONATHAN, ED. "Investing in Solar Energy: Recommendations for the U.S. Department of Energy's Research and Development Budget for Renewable Energy Technologies FY 1992–1994." 2nd ed. Washington, D.C.: Public Citizen, March 1991. (Available from Public Citizen, 215 Pennsylvania Avenue, SE, Washington, DC 20003 [202] 546-4996. Price: $10.00)

BEVINGTON, RICK, AND ARTHUR H. ROSENFELD. "Energy for Buildings and Homes." *Scientific American* September 1990, pp. 77–86.

BOWLER, SUE. "The First Steps Out of the Greenhouse." *New Scientist* February 16, 1991, p. 45.

DREYFUS, DANIEL A., AND ANNE B. ASHBY. "Fueling Our Global Future." *Environment* May 1990, pp. 17–20 +.

DWORETZKY, TOM. "Perpetual Power: Can We Develop a Sane Energy Strategy for the Future?" *Omni* May 1991, p. 34–38.

EFKEN, DAVID. "Pushing the Power of Alternative Energy Resources." Washington, D.C.: Public Citizen, April 1987. (Available from Public Citizen, 215 Pennsylvania Avenue, SE, Washington, DC 20003 [202] 546-4996. Price: $2.00)

"Energy." Washington, D.C.: Greenpeace Action, 1991.

"Environmental Taxes." *Solar Today* May/June 1991, p. 25.

"Fact Sheet: The National Energy Strategy." Washington, D.C.: The White House, Office of the Press Secretary, February 20, 1991.

GOODWIN, IRWIN. "An Energy Strategy for All Seasons Gets Rough Treatment in Congress." *Physics Today* July 1991, pp. 47–48.

GREEN, SHIRLEY M. Letter from Green (special assistant to the president for presidential messages and correspondence) to the author, April 24, 1991.

"The Greenhouse Effect." Washington, D.C.: Greenpeace, 1992.

LEE, WILLIAM S. "Energy for Our Globe's People." *Environment* September 1990, pp. 12–15 +.

MACKENZIE, DEBORA. "Energy Answers for North and South." *New Scientist* February 16, 1991, pp. 48–51.

———. "Swedes Step Up Search for Alternative Energy." *New Scientist* January 26, 1991, p. 20.

National Energy Strategy: Powerful Ideas for America. Washington, D.C.: U.S. Government Printing Office, 1991.

Nixon, Will. "Energy for the Next Century." *E Magazine* May/June 1991, pp. 31–39.

Pool, Robert. "More Free Market, Less Regulation, Bush Asks." *Nature* February 28, 1991, p. 729.

Public Citizen. "A Sustainable Energy Future—Principles and Goals for a National Energy Strategy." Washington, D.C.: Public Citizen, 1990. (Available from Public Citizen, 215 Pennsylvania Avenue, SE, Washington, DC 20003 [202] 546-4996. Price: $0.75)

Salaff, Stephen. "Sustainable Strategies in Ontario." *Independent Energy* September 1990, pp. 70–71.

Sheinkopf, Kenneth. "The Clean Air Act: A Preview." *Independent Energy* July/August 1990, pp. 71–72.

Sklar, Scott. "A Renewable Energy Strategy." *Independent Energy* February 1990, pp. 49–51.

Watts, Susan. "Fresh Threat to Renewable Energy Projects." *New Scientist* August 18, 1990, p. 13.

GENERAL

Baker, Hugh D. "Tapping the Public Power Market." *Independent Energy* October 1990, pp. 64–66.

Bevington, Rick, and Arthur H. Rosenfeld. "Energy for Buildings and Homes." *Scientific American* September 1990, pp. 77–86.

Bowler, Sue. "The First Steps Out of the Greenhouse." *New Scientist* February 16, 1991, pp. 45–47.

Brower, Michael. *Cool Energy: The Renewable Solution to Global Warming.* Cambridge, Mass.: Union of Concerned Scientists, 1990.

Buderi, Robert, et al. "Conservation Power." *Business Week* September 16, 1991, pp. 86–92.

Byrne, Jeanne. "Mythbusters #5: Renewable Energy." Washington, D.C.: Safe Energy Communication Council, 1990.

California Energy Commission. *California's Energy Plan: California Energy Commission 1991 Biennial Report.* Sacramento: California Energy Commission, 1991.

———. *Electricity Report.* Sacramento: California Energy Commission, 1990.

———. *Energy Technology Status Report: Report Summary.* Sacramento: California Energy Commission, 1990.

Davis, Ged R. "Energy for Planet Earth." *Scientific American* September 1990, pp. 55–62.

Energy for Islands. Proceedings of an international conference organized by the Society for Underwater Technology. London: Graham and Trotman, 1988.

Eronn, Robert. "Ecological Living in Sweden—Ideas and Practical Experience." *Current Sweden* no. 378, May 1991, pp. 2–8.

Fedoruk, Nicholas. "Mythbusters #6: Energy Efficiency," Washington, D.C.: Safe Energy Communication Council, 1990.

FICKETT, ARNOLD P., ET AL. "Efficient Use of Electricity." *Scientific American* September 1990, pp. 65–74.

FLANIGAN, TED. "Energy Efficiency: Key To Solving Economic, Environmental Problems." *Forum for Applied Research and Public Policy* Spring 1991, pp. 55–59.

FULKERSON, WILLIAM, ET AL. "Energy from Fossil Fuels." *Scientific American* September 1990, pp. 129–35.

GAS RESEARCH INSTITUTE. *GRI Baseline Projection of U.S. Energy Supply and Demand, 1992 Edition.* Chicago, Ill.: Gas Research Institute, 1991.

GRUBB, M. J. "The Cinderella options." *Energy Policy* October 1990, pp. 711–25.

HUBBARD, HAROLD M. "The Real Cost of Energy." *Scientific American* April 1991, pp. 36–42.

IDAHO NATIONAL ENGINEERING LABORATORY, ET AL. *The Potential of Renewable Energy.* Interlaboratory white paper prepared for the Office of Policy, Planning and Analysis. Washington, D.C.: U.S. Department of Energy, 1990.

INTERNATIONAL ENERGY AGENCY (IEA). *Renewable Sources of Energy.* Paris: OECD/IEA, 1987.

MINISTRY OF ENERGY, DANISH ENERGY AGENCY. "The Danish Contribution Towards a Sustainable Development." Copenhagen: Ministry of Energy, 1990.

MINISTRY OF THE ENVIRONMENT (SWEDEN). "Swedish Environmental Legislation." Stockholm: Ministry of the Environment, 1990.

NICKLAS, MICHAEL. "Societal Costs of Energy." *ASES 1989 Roundtable: Societal Costs of Energy.* Boulder, Colo.: American Solar Energy Society, 1989.

PELAYO, MOISES. "Alternative Generation Manual." San Francisco: California Public Utilities Commission, Division of Ratepayer Advocates, Energy Resources Branch, 1989.

POIRIER, JEAN-LOUIS, AND BILL MEADE. "Assessing the World Market." *Independent Energy* January 1990, pp. 49–52.

RADER, NANCY. "Power Surge." Washington, D.C.: Public Citizen, 1989. (Available from Public Citizen, 215 Pennsylvania Avenue, SE, Washington, DC 20003 [202] 546–4996. Price: $10.00)

RADER, NANCY, AND KEN BOSSONG. "Renewable Energy Poised to Triple by Year 2000." Washington, D.C.: Public Citizen, 1991. (Available from Public Citizen, 215 Pennsylvania Avenue, SE, Washington, DC 20003 [202] 546–4996. Price: $1.75)

REDDY, AMULYA K. N., AND JOSE GOLDEMBERG. "Energy for the Developing World." *Scientific American* September 1990, pp. 111–18.

ROSS, MARC H., AND DANIEL STEINMEYER. "Energy for Industry." *Scientific American* September 1990, pp. 89–98.

SAFE ENERGY COMMUNICATION COUNCIL (SECC). "Renewable Energy: It's Ready Now (ENfacts)." Washington, D.C.: Safe Energy Communication Council, 1990.

SHEA, CYNTHIA POLLOCK. *Renewable Energy: Today's Contribution, Tomorrow's Promise.* Washington, D.C.: Worldwatch Institute, 1988.

SKLAR, SCOTT. "U.S. Biomass Industry Must Set the Record Straight." *Biologue* September 1991, p. 3.

———. Testimony of Sklar (in his capacity as executive director, Solar Energy Industries Association) before the House Appropriations Committee Subcommittee on Energy & Water Development, Washington, D.C., April 9, 1991.

———. Testimony of Sklar (in his capacity as executive director, U.S. Export Council for Renewable Energy) before the House Appropriations Committee Subcommittee on Foreign Operations FY '92 Appropriations: AID, OPEC, TDP, Washington, D.C., June 25, 1991.

SOLAR ENERGY RESEARCH AND EDUCATION FOUNDATION. "Renewable Energy: Facts and Figures." Washington, D.C.: Solar Energy Research and Education Foundation, 1991.

SOLAR ENERGY RESEARCH INSTITUTE (SERI). "Conservation and Renewable Energy Technologies for Buildings." Golden, Colo.: SERI, 1991.

———. "Conservation and Renewable Energy Technologies for Transportation." Golden, Colo.: SERI, 1990.

———. "CORECT 1990—Committee on Renewable Energy Commerce and Trade." Golden, Colo.: SERI, 1991.

———. "Energy for Today—Renewable Energy." Golden, Colo.: SERI, 1990.

———. "Energy Storage and Distribution Program Summary, Vol. 1: Overview FY 1989." Golden, Golo.: SERI, 1990.

———. "Programs in Renewable Energy, Fiscal Year 1990." Golden, Colo.: SERI, 1990.

THOMPSON, RENEE. "Electricity in the Making." *PG&E Progress* August 1991, pp. 2–3.

TILLANDER, STAFFAN. "Sweden and International Environmental Cooperation." Stockholm: Ministry of Foreign Affairs (Sweden), 1991.

U.S. AGENCY FOR INTERNATIONAL DEVELOPMENT (U.S. AID). "Improving the Quality of Life with Renewable Energy." Washington, D.C.: U.S. AID, 1990.

———. "Renewable Energy for Agriculture and Health." Washington, D.C.: U.S. AID, 1988.

U.S. DEPARTMENT OF ENERGY (U.S. DOE). "Alternatives to Air as Heat Sources for Heat Pumps." 2nd ed. Washington, D.C.: U.S. DOE, 1989.

———. "Learning About Renewable Energy." 2nd ed. Washington, D.C.: U.S. DOE, 1989.

———. "Renewable Energy: An Overview." 3rd ed. Washington, D.C.: U.S. DOE, 1990.

———. "Characterization of U.S. Energy Resources and Reserves." Washington, D.C.: U.S. DOE, 1989.

U.S. EXPORT COUNCIL FOR RENEWABLE ENERGY (US/ECRE). "Improving the Quality of Life with Renewable Energy Highlights of U.S. Private-Sector Applications in USAID-Assisted Countries." Arlington, Va: US/ECRE, 1990.

———. "Renewable Energy for the World, 1990." Arlington, Va.: US/ECRE, 1990.

WATSON, ROBERT K. "Office Space Designed for Energy Savings." *Forum for Applied Research and Public Policy* Spring 1991, pp. 60–64.

WOODWARD, BRIAN. "Australia's Race for Clean Cars." *New Scientist* February 9, 1991, p. 31.

Index

NOV 2	DATE DUE		
MAY 0 5 1995			
5-7-97			
APR 09 2001			
12-13-06			
10/28/12			